LEARNING DISABILITIES

Penny Hutchins Paquette
Cheryl Gerson Tuttle

It Happened to Me, No. 1

The Scarecrow Press, Inc.
Lanham, Maryland, and Oxford
2003

SCARECROW PRESS, INC.

Published in the United States of America
by Scarecrow Press, Inc.
A Member of the Rowman & Littlefield Publishing Group
4720 Boston Way, Lanham, Maryland 20706
www.scarecrowpress.com

PO Box 317
Oxford
OX2 9RU, UK

British Library Cataloguing in Publication Information Available

Library of Congress Cataloging-in-Publication Data Available

Paquette, Penny Hutchins.
   Learning disabilities : the ultimate teen guide / Penny Hutchins Paquette,
Cheryl Gerson Tuttle.
      p. cm. — (It happened to me ; no. 1)
   Includes bibliographical references and index.
   ISBN 0-8108-4261-0 (alk. paper)
   1. Learning disabled teenagers—Education—United States—Handbooks,
manuals, etc. 2. Learning disabilities—Handbooks, manuals, etc. I. Title: The
ultimate teen guide. II. Tuttle, Cheryl Gerson. III. Title. IV. Series.
   LC4704.74 .P37 2003
   371.9—dc21   2002017588

For all students with learning disabilities
—PP

For Henry
—CT

Contents

Acknowledgments

When we began working on this book, we reached out to those around us who had a particular expertise to share. Specialists who help students with learning disabilities each day were willing to share their experiences and ideas to help us develop this book. Thanks to Marblehead High School Special Education Chairperson Kathy Glennon for getting us started.

To Dr. Ronna Fried and Dr. John Secor for sharing their special expertise about the brain.

To directors of special education services here in our home state: Sandra Baer, coordinator of Academic Services for Students with Disabilities, Tufts University; Eileen Berger, director of the Office for Students with Disabilities, Salem State College; Lisa Igiri, director of the Program for Advancement of Learning, Curry College; and Christopher Kennedy, coordinator of Disability Services, Babson College. To David R. Leslie, director of the Threshold Program at Lesley University, a special thanks for providing information to help young people make the transition from high school to further education and for confirming our beliefs that educational opportunities are available for young people with a wide range of learning disabilities.

Thank you to all the students who helped us with this book, and particularly to a special group of students at Babson College and at the Threshold Program at Lesley College, for giving us a student's-eye view into what it is like to have a learning disability.

Thanks to Cornelius H. Bull, Center for INTERIM Programs, for showing us the many programs and experiences available for young people who are looking for "time on" after high school.

Much appreciation to the reference librarians at our local library, Abbot Public Library, who tracked down every article and reference book we weren't able to retrieve ourselves. They are an invaluable resource.

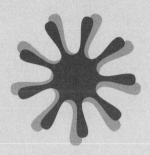

Introduction

K eith knew he had a learning disability. He had trouble understanding his social studies textbook. Even when he did his
homework, he couldn't always answer the quiz questions the next
day. Does this sound familiar? When teachers in the resource room
taught him new strategies, he was able to pass this hard course.

As a sophomore in high school, Carrie knew that her parents met
with her teachers and that they talked about her. She knew her parents
weren't always happy with the results of those meetings and that they
sometimes had to go to another meeting before they were satisfied.
What Carrie didn't know was exactly what happened in those meetings and what all those people said about her there. Could this be you?

Like most students with learning disabilities, Keith and Carrie knew
a lot about the things that gave them trouble in school. They knew
which classes were easy for them and which gave them a hard time.
They knew which teachers helped them learn and which didn't help
them. They knew what time of day they learned the best and they knew
that early mornings were the worst for them. Keith knew his parents
wanted him to go to the same university his father attended, but he

wasn't so sure that was what he wanted to do after high school. Carrie's parents didn't think she could get into college, but she wanted to go away to school like her friends. Unfortunately, Keith and Carrie never shared this information with the group of people who made decisions about their education. Keith and Carrie are probably a lot like you.

As we talked to teenagers like Keith and Carrie, we realized that most of them needed more information. Though these students knew they had a learning disability and could give us a few examples of symptoms, they couldn't always tell us the name of the disability or what educational plan was in place to help them learn. Some didn't even know if they had an educational plan. Most couldn't tell their classroom teacher what kinds of changes could make learning easier for them.

Many of the students we talked to hoped to go to college after high school, but few knew what the requirements were for the colleges they were interested in or whether they would be able to do college-level work. Some students knew about the educational laws that protect them as high school students, but few knew that the laws change once they go to college, where schools are obliged to provide *reasonable accommodations*, but not individualized education plans. Most were interested in new technologies, but didn't know about options that might help them learn while they were in high school or a year or two down the road when they were ready for college.

Though a few resented their mothers and/or fathers for playing such a large role in their high school life, most were happy to let their parents handle anything that had to do with school.

Parents can be (and most often are) your greatest support, but as you get older, you need to take some responsibility for your own education. Why should you become involved? Because students who are the most involved are the most likely to be successful not only in high school but in college and on the job as well. Although many of the teenagers we talked to didn't have a clue, those who knew the most about their disabilities were the most successful.

If you haven't already realized it, learning disabilities can create problems not only at home and in school but in social situations as well. Have you ever felt you just didn't fit in? Are you ever at a loss for words when you are around someone you like? Have you ever turned to alcohol or drugs to make you feel better? Most teenagers have had these experiences, but for students with learning disabilities, issues with friends are even more complicated. This book can't make you the most popular student in your school and it can't make you the smartest kid in your class, but it will help you in your day-to-day life. We have gathered some tips from successful college students who took the time to look back on their high school years. They remember quite well how it feels to be a high school student with learning disabilities and they have shared their thoughts and feelings to help you better understand the challenges you face.

They often told us that one of the most important factors in your success will be your ability to understand your specific learning disability, to make decisions for yourself, to ask for what you need, and to create and carry out plans that will help you reach your goals. We have gathered information from students, from high school guidance counselors, from disability services coordinators at colleges, and from other professionals who have experience with learning disabilities. We have pulled that information together and present it in a way to help guide you through the next few years.

You may need all of the chapters in this book or you might just need one or two. Though teachers often advise reading a book from the beginning to the end, we realize you probably don't want to do that. Read through the table of contents and choose the sections that interest you. We recommend that you have a thorough understanding of your learning disability, so if you don't know how to define and explain your learning problems, start with the first chapters. If you are a person who likes to know the answers to the *why* of learning disabilities, chapter 2 provides information about the brain and current research on how your brain affects the way you learn.

All students in their teens should be actively involved in their Individualized Educational Plan (IEP). If you don't know what that is or you don't know what yours says, you need chapter 10. By the time you are in seventh or eighth grade and certainly by the time you are in high school, you will also need the chapter on transitions (chapter 11). This will help you get ready for your life after high school. Though that may be a few years away, you need to start planning for that time now.

If you are unsure about what you want to do after high school, chapters 13 and 14 can help you think about that.

Maybe you have trouble knowing what to say to teachers or to your parents. Or maybe you have no trouble saying things to them, but get in trouble when you do. We have included sample "things to say" in the book to help you express your needs and goals in ways that will make adults sit up (and sometimes shut up) and listen.

The subject of learning disabilities comes with special words that can confuse almost anyone. Though these words help educators and lawyers, they are more complicated than necessary. If you find the language confusing (and most people do), there is a glossary at the end of the book that puts these terms into understandable language.

If you want to learn more about your specific learning disability or would like to read about other teenagers who have learning disabilities, a list of print and Internet resources is at the end of every chapter and in the back of the book.

We wrote this book for you. We have drawn from our professional experiences, the most recent research, and the best advice from teenagers like you to give you what you need. This book is not for your parents. If there are things you want them to know, show them those sections of the book.

The most important factor in your success does not come from your teachers, your parents, or your advisors. Though these people are very important, you won't succeed unless *you* become involved. The person who can have the greatest impact on your success is you.

Learning Disabilities: An Overview

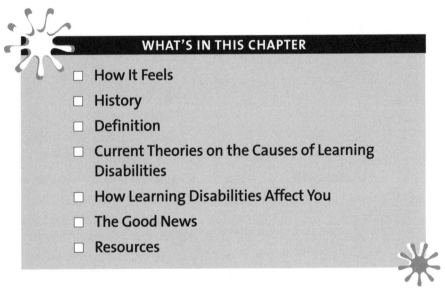

WHAT'S IN THIS CHAPTER

- ☐ How It Feels
- ☐ History
- ☐ Definition
- ☐ Current Theories on the Causes of Learning Disabilities
- ☐ How Learning Disabilities Affect You
- ☐ The Good News
- ☐ Resources

How It Feels

Young people with learning disabilities (LD) say they feel frustrated, lonely, angry, stupid, and confused. Because no two people are alike and because there are a number of very different learning disabilities, students who struggle with LD display a variety of symptoms.

They hope they won't have to read aloud in front of the class. They pray they won't have to give an oral report. They fear getting lost. They cringe at the idea of an essay test. They hope they won't say something stupid. They hope they can find their homework.

Written reports are nightmares. Math is torture. Making friends is impossible. Failure is often the focus of the day.

The one thing most students with LD have in common is frustration. They know they are smart, but they feel stupid. It sounds impossible, but if you are a student with a learning disability, you know the feeling.

History

Young people have struggled with learning for as long as adults have tried to teach them, and educators have been searching for the reasons for those struggles for just as long. If you are a teenager with a learning disability today, you know how hard it can be to learn new lessons. You probably receive some help with your schoolwork and you may spend some time in a special education classroom designed to help students with learning problems. You may think that is a

> My Mom and I were getting into fights trying to figure out what I had and how to deal with it. . . . I used to think that everything was my fault.
> —Laura, a college student

> I was perceived as stupid, and I felt stupid and ashamed of myself. Those feelings and self-perceptions are sometimes even issues I deal with today.
> —Jonathan Mooney, executive director of Eye-to-Eye, a nonprofit company matching college students with learning disabilities with elementary school students with related problems. Mooney has written about his experiences with learning disabilities in his book *Learning Outside the Lines.*

drag, but if you look back in history, you can begin to appreciate how fortunate you are, despite your learning disability.

Although definitions and explanations of learning disabilities have been researched for more than 100 years, the most disturbing historical information comes in the treatment of young people with learning difficulties. Just fifty years ago, young children with learning disabilities were misunderstood and educationally mistreated. It was not uncommon in the 1950s to have children with learning disabilities shut away in classrooms far from the normal activities of a school. Basement rooms, rooms without windows, and isolated classrooms were all commonplace. Students with learning disabilities were often instructed in the same classrooms as children who were mentally retarded, those with emotional problems, or other physical or emotional disabilities. Students were punished, laughed at, expelled, beaten, ridiculed, ostracized, humiliated, and/or held back until they were years older than their classmates. Many never graduated from high school. Few went on to college. Educators just didn't understand the complexity of learning disabilities and parents didn't understand either.

According to the National Center for Learning Disabilities, Samuel Kirk first used the term "learning disability" in 1962 to describe those with *average* or *better* intelligence who had difficulty with basic academic skills. Though the term first came into use in the early 1960s, educators and psychologists recognized that children had difficulty learning long before that and most believed the learning problems were caused by injuries to the brain.

Believe it or not, studies of reading problems date back to the late 1800s. At that time, W. Pringle Morgan, an English ophthalmologist, created the term "word blindness" to describe those who had difficulty learning to read. Even the term "dyslexia" was used as far back as 1887 when Rudolf Berlin used it to describe his patients who had difficulty reading.

In 1928, Samuel Orton, a neurologist from Iowa, identified children who confused some letters, *b* or *d*, for example. Others could read pages held up to a mirror, and some did mirror writing. He was among the first to believe that this reading difficulty might be caused by faulty brain connections.

Problems with writing were recognized as early as 1868 when neuroanatomist Henry Charlton Bastian observed deficits in written language, calling the problem "agraphia."

Physician Heinrich Hoffmann described hyperactive children in the mid-1800s in his illustrated story "Fidgety Philipp," in which he described a young boy who just couldn't sit still. By 1907, Herman Oppenheim reported his experience with children who exhibited many of the symptoms associated with Attention Deficit Hyperactivity Disorder (ADHD) today.

Heinz Werner, a psychologist, and his associate, Alfred A. Strauss, a neuropsychiatrist, did pioneering work in the 1930s and 1940s. They referred to children with learning problems as "brain injured," and believed they were injured before, during, or after birth. Their studies distinguished between young people who were "brain injured" and those who were retarded.

The controversy over stimulant medications dates back to the 1930s. In 1937, medical professionals at Bradley Hospital in Providence, Rhode Island, began treating what they called "hyperactive" children with stimulant medications. The doctors said this treatment was "better than whacking them on the seat of the pants." Charles Bradley and Maurice Loffer began documenting the benefits and the side effects of treating children with attention deficits with stimulants. By the 1980s, attention deficit disorder (ADD) was clearly defined and recognized as a specific disorder. The controversy over stimulant medications continues today.

By the 1950s and early 1960s, the term *brain-injured* was no longer in favor, and researchers began calling children with learning problems *perceptually handicapped*. Still later, the term *minimal brain dysfunction syndrome* was used.

The Story of Fidgety Philipp

Heinrich Hoffmann wrote about a little boy who couldn't sit still in "The Story of Fidgety Philipp," one of the stories in *Der Struwwelpeter*, first published in the mid-1800s. He wrote:

> See the naughty, restless child,
> Growing still more rude and wild,
> Till his chair falls over quite.
> Philipp screams with all his might,
> Catches at the cloth, but then
> That makes matters worse again.
> Down upon the ground they fall,
> Glasses, bread, knives, forks and all.
> How Mamma did fret and frown,
> When she saw them tumbling down!
> And Papa made such a face!
> Philipp is in sad disgrace.

Illustration by Heinrich Hoffmann from *Der Struwwelpeter: Oder lustige Geschichten und drollige Bilder fur Kinder von 3–6 Jahren* (Frankfurt am Main: Literarische Anstalt von Rutten & Loning, 1900)

Beginning in the mid-1960s, the federal government began providing funds for the education of children with disabilities, and by the 1970s had mandated a *free and appropriate education,* providing opportunities for learning disabled children to receive the services they needed in the regular classroom, sometimes with additional support outside the classroom.

In the 1990s, the Individuals with Disabilities Act provided legislation calling for assistive technological devices, and later for the inclusion of services for college students. If you are interested in these laws, the rights they mandate, and how they affect you, read more about them in chapter 12.

HISTORICAL REVIEW

Late 1800s

Morgan uses the term *word blindness.*
Bastian uses the term *agraphia.*
Berlin uses the term *dyslexia.*
Hoffmann writes *Fidgety Philipp.*

Early 1900s

Oppenheim reports ADHD-like symptoms.

1920s–1930s

Strauss and Werner blame *brain injuries* for learning
    problems.
Orton suspects reading problems might be caused by
    improper connections in the brain.

1930s

"Hyperactive" children are first treated with stimulants.
Loffer and Bradley document benefits and effects of
    stimulants.

1950s–1960s

Children called *perceptually handicapped*. The term *minimal brain dysfunction* is also used.

Kirk proposes the term *learning disability*.

Association for Children with Learning Disabilities founded.

Federal government provides funds for education of children with disabilities.

1970s

Legislation mandates *a free and appropriate* education for students with learning disabilities.

1980s

ADHD is recognized as specific disorder.

1990s

Special technologies and accommodations for college students are mandated.

Today

Research continues in areas of heredity and brain activity.

Definition

Today the term "learning disability" is used to describe any number of problems that make it difficult for people to learn. It is a term used to describe people who have a variety of learning problems that affect storing, processing, or producing information. When these problems create gaps between ability and performance, they are called learning disabilities. Because ADHD can get in the way of learning, we are including it in our discussion of learning disabilities.

If you have a learning disability, your intelligence is in the average to above-average range, yet your performance in a particular area falls below your IQ. The National Institute of Mental Health (NIMH) explains that a learning disability is not a "diagnosis in the same sense as chickenpox or mumps . . . but rather a broad term that covers a pool of possible causes, symptoms, treatments, and outcomes." Unfortunately, there is no vaccine to prevent or to cure learning disabilities yet.

Depending on your specific disability, you may have problems reading, speaking, writing, working with numbers, or organizing your thoughts. Or you may have problems sitting still and paying attention. You may have problems taking tests, or you could have problems in social situations. And you may have problems in more than one area. The area or areas of difficulty help identify specific learning disabilities as described in the next chapters.

Does this sound like you? You are smart enough. You have at least average intelligence—though you don't always feel smart. You are very good at some things, but other areas give you a lot of trouble. Your performance doesn't match your potential.

You've heard this kind of thing so often you want to go out and buy earplugs: "He is capable of doing better." Or, "She doesn't do as well as she should." Or, "If only he would try harder."

You are, in fact, probably working harder than most of your friends, and you are not alone. Look around at the next school event. If there are over 100 students there, between five and twenty of them will have a learning disability of some kind. Between 1997 and 1998, 2.7 million students received special education services. This large number is related both to a better understanding of learning disabilities and to changes in the laws governing how students with disabilities are treated in school. Over the past forty years, changes in legislation have helped children receive better educational services than ever before. If you are in high school now, you have probably benefited from that kind of help since elementary school or junior high.

Current Theories on the Causes of Learning Disabilities

The words "may be" are often found in lists of causes of learning disabilities. Though research on learning disabilities is ongoing, experts still don't know exactly what causes them. Most believe that learning disabilities are caused by a problem in the central nervous system. Recent research on the workings of the brain indicates there may be malfunctions or misfires between or among areas of the brain. You can read more about this in chapter 2. Heredity also appears to play a role in several specific learning disabilities

Other factors that may contribute to learning disabilities include birth defects, injuries, premature delivery, low birth weight, long labor, malnutrition, and lead poisoning. Learning disabilities may also be influenced by factors before birth, including alcohol or drug abuse, or injury or illness during pregnancy,

As research in this area is moving ahead rapidly, we may eventually know what causes learning disabilities, but you may never know exactly what caused your particular LD. What you should know is that it does little good to blame others for your learning problems. As a young adult, you need to recognize them, take responsibility for them, and take the actions that will help you succeed. What you need to know is that you can learn to compensate for these shortcomings and you can excel, even though your learning disability will not go away and it can't be *cured*.

How Learning Disabilities Affect You

Academic Problems

Students with learning disabilities usually require help in some academic areas in school. Those with more serious learning problems may need specialized instruction outside the regular classroom. Those with less serious problems may only need occasional support. You may need after-school support for homework. You may need to have a teacher read through your written work before you hand it in. You may need help in keeping organized. In the best of situations, special educators help you learn the strategies you will need to be successful on your own once you finish high school.

A chapter in this book is devoted to each specific learning disability, and the lists that follow give a general overview of difficulties you may experience. Glance though the categories and see if one of these areas gives you more trouble than others. If you aren't sure exactly how to categorize your specific learning problems, this may help you find the terms you need to describe the problems you face. Being able to describe your learning problem is crucial in coming to terms with your learning disability and in getting the help you need. Use this guide to help you decide which chapter or chapters you should read for specific information about your particular learning disability.

Attention

Trouble with focusing and/or staying focused on work

* Easily distracted
* Problems with giving attention to details
* Problems with handling multiple tasks
* Problems with following instructions
* Poor impulse control: acting and/or speaking without thinking

* Hyperactivity
* Daydreaming
* Impatience
* Restlessness

If this list looks familiar, read chapter 3 (Attention Deficit Hyperactivity Disorder).

Communication Skills

* Trouble with written or spoken language
* Trouble with getting thoughts on paper
* Poor grammar
* Poor spelling
* Problems with copying information from text or blackboard
* Writing slowly
* Poor handwriting
* Understanding spoken language
* Trouble with saying what you mean
* Trouble with using correct grammar
* Trouble with understanding or talking about unfamiliar subjects
* Trouble with telling a story in the right order (trouble telling jokes)
* Trouble with following spoken instructions

If these difficulties sound familiar, read chapters 5 and 6 on dysgraphia and dyslexia.

Math

* Problems with basic computation
* Problems with paying attention to problem-solving tasks

✳ Problems with finding the correct place on worksheets

✳ Trouble with lining up columns

✳ Number confusion (6 and 9, for example, or 17 and 71)

✳ Problems with understanding the basic signs, +, -, %, etc.

✳ Problems with concepts of time and direction

✳ Problems with balancing a checkbook

✳ Problems with making change

✳ Problems with music

✳ Poor coordination

✳ Problems with remembering the steps or sequences for sports

✳ Problems with keeping score

✳ Problems with estimating

If these symptoms apply to you, read the dyscalculia chapter (chapter 4). Some problems in math are related to nonverbal learning disabilities. Read more about that below.

Nonverbal

✳ Lack of coordination and/or balance

✳ Fine motor skills problems, including drawing, writing, copying, etc.

✳ May focus on details and fail to see the big picture

✳ Inability to understand body language

✳ Problems with social instincts

✳ Inability to read the intentions of others

✳ Difficulty with conversations

✳ Getting lost

✳ Problems with understanding maps, charts, graphs, etc.

If you have problems in these areas, read chapter 8 (Nonverbal Learning Disability).

Organization

✳ Problems with organizing in all areas

✳ Problems with managing time

✳ Problems with getting started; procrastination

✳ Problems with remembering school work

✳ Losing papers, books, car keys, etc.

Problems with organization are common in most students with learning disabilities. Check the index under *organization* for specific page references.

Reading

✳ Reading slowly

✳ Problems with spelling

✳ Problems with summarizing and outlining

✳ Poor vocabulary

✳ Poor comprehension and recall of information

✳ Problems with taking notes

✳ Problems with concentrating while reading

✳ Problems with organizing and completing written projects

✳ Trouble identifying themes or main topics

✳ Problems with answering open-ended questions

✳ Reading words or letters out of sequence

✳ Skipping words or lines

✳ Difficulty with abstract concepts

✳ Problems with completing assignments

If you have problems in these areas, read the information on dyslexia in chapter 6.

Social Issues

"Retard," "dummy," "loser." You've probably heard those expressions at least once during your school years. The terms are not only inappropriate, they are just plain wrong. Remember, the very definition of learning disabilities states you are of *at least* average intelligence. Though it is difficult to ignore hurtful taunts, you can at least acknowledge that they are not true.

Cruelty from others is something most young people with learning disabilities need to deal with. Unfortunately, some of the problems teenagers have with friendships are at least indirectly related to their own behavior. Making friends is sometimes a problem. One of the major factors in this area of concern comes with impulse control. If you find yourself saying the wrong thing at the wrong time, you are not entirely different from most teenagers.

Some teenagers, however, have poor impulse control. If you often act without thinking, or find yourself in situations where you have done something you know is inappropriate but can't figure out why you did it, you may have ADHD, or attention deficit hyperactivity disorder. Short attention span, restlessness, inappropriate behavior, impulsivity, thoughtless, and careless behavior are all symptoms of ADHD. If you are thoughtless and impulsive and can't pay attention to what your friends are saying, it is not surprising that you have problems in social situations. Like all learning disabilities, however, there are strategies to help you in these areas. Medications may also help. For more information, read chapter 3 on ADHD.

Much of what goes on between young adults in a social setting is related to watching how others behave and copying that behavior to fit in. Some young people can't do that. These teenagers may have non-verbal learning disorders. There is more about this disorder in chapter 8 (Nonverbal Learning Disability).

Depression

Problems with learning and with friends can lead to depression. If you are having feelings of hope-lessness or helplessness or are displaying the following symptoms, don't ignore them. Talk to an adult that you trust.

✳ Profound sadness or tearful most of the time

✳ Irritability

✳ Excessive restlessness or lack of energy

✳ Not caring about anything

✳ Problems with sleeping too little or too much

THE ROLLER COASTER OF LIFE

The Roller Coaster glides
through the air
And soars up in the sky.

But as life has its ups
and downs,
So does the roller
coaster.

Life has its fears,
its joys and sorrows.

The roller coaster is
almighty and
powerful.
You never know what
direction it could go—
up or down.

Just so life—you never
know what your
future will hold

From one day to the next.

—Molly Gonzalez,
a young adult with
learning disabilities

He had trouble learning to write. He found grade-school calculations impossible. He had trouble with reading in history and in English. His teachers challenged him to work harder and called him lazy He says he was a student with a "questionable future." Though he wanted to be a doctor, he had trouble getting into medical school.

Today, Dr. Fred J. Epstein is the director of the Institute for Neurology and Neurosurgery (INN), a state-of-the-art diagnosis and treatment center for patients with neurological disorders at Beth Israel Medical Center in New York. He is a pioneer in the treatment of spinal cord tumors, having developed unprecedented techniques for the neurosurgical removal of brain stem and spinal cord tumors. In addition to his surgical work, he also strives to create a "healing environment" for his patients and their families. The transition from a classroom "underachiever" to an operating room genius was not an easy one.

In an ABC.com interview following a *Nightline* appearance, Dr. Epstein said that when he was a student, he and others with learning disabilities were viewed as unintelligent. "The greatest sadness was that we viewed ourselves the same way," said Epstein. Students with learning disabilities went undiagnosed in those days. In fact, Dr. Epstein did not recognize his problems in school as disability related until his own daughter was tested and diagnosed with learning disabilities.

He credits his determination and his willingness to work harder than other students with his success. He calls his work ethic a simple one. "I would put in many more hours studying than my friends would to accomplish the same end. I will never forget how my friends were all very surprised that anyone could work as hard as I did for such mediocre results." As a result, he was willing to reach and to work for the seemingly impossible to fulfill his ambitions.

Photo by Fran Collin

✳ Eating problems

✳ Feelings of despair

✳ Feelings of low self-esteem or worthlessness

✳ Feelings of shame

✳ Inability to think clearly or concentrate

✳ Social withdrawal, no longer enjoying favorite activities

✳ Excessive guilt

✳ Suicidal or self-injurious thoughts

It is not unusual for teenagers with learning disabilities to have these feelings. Professionals can help you.

The Good News

Learning disabilities often create problems that make school difficult, but those with learning disabilities also have skills and talents that far outweigh academic weaknesses. Today, learning disabilities are discovered earlier than ever (some new research predicts LD in newborns); as a result, students can receive the help they need in learning to compensate for their areas of weakness. There are successful people in all areas who have struggled with learning disabilities but have found tremendous success as adults. Artists, actors, athletes, craftspeople, entrepreneurs, explorers, investment advisors, lawyers, scientists, writers, and people in every field have refused to let their learning disabilities hold them back. Comments from them are included in the chapters covering specific disabilities. Read on and be inspired.

This chapter has given you a brief overview of learning disabilities, including a brief history. Here are the highlights—the things we would like you to remember.

REMEMBER
- You have at least average intelligence—you are probably even brighter than average. Though you may have areas of weakness, you also have areas of strength.
- Causes of learning disabilities are still uncertain, though most likely are related to brain structure or function.
- Progress has been made and will continue to be made in the understanding of learning disabilities.
- Specific disabilities have specific symptoms and specific strategies for coping.
- Learning disabilities can affect both academic and social situations.
- You need to learn as much as possible about your specific learning problem by reading more about it in the appropriate chapter.
- Successful people in all walks of life have learning disabilities.

Resources

Council for Learning Disabilities (CLD)
P.O. Box 40303
Overland Park, KS 66204
(913) 492-8755

Lauren, Jill. *Succeeding with LD: 20 True Stories about Real People with LD*. Minneapolis, MN: Free Spirit, 1997.

LDOnline
http://www.ldonline.org

LDTeens
http://www.ldteens.org

Sponsored by the New York Branch of the International
  Dyslexia Association
(212) 691-1930

Learning Disabilities Association of America (LDA)
  4156 Library Road
  Pittsburgh, PA 15234
  (412) 341-1515
  http://www.ldanatl.org/

National Center for Learning Disabilities
  381 Park Avenue South, Suite 1401
  New York, NY 10016
  (888) 575-7373 (toll free)
  http://www.ncld.org

The National Information Center for Children and Youth with
  Disabilities (NICHCY)
  P. O. Box 1492
  Washington, DC 20013
  (800) 695-0285
  http://www.nichcy.org

National Institute of Mental Health (NIMH)
  6001 Executive Blvd. Room 8184
  Bethesda, MD 20892-9663
  (301) 443-4513
  www.nimh.nih.gov

Schwab Foundation for Learning
  1650 South Amphlett Blvd., Suite 300
  San Mateo, CA 94402
  (800) 230-0988
  http://www.schwablearning.org/

Your Brain

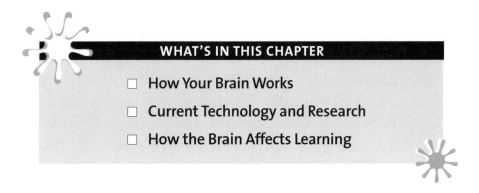

WHAT'S IN THIS CHAPTER

☐ **How Your Brain Works**

☐ **Current Technology and Research**

☐ **How the Brain Affects Learning**

Think of a large symphony orchestra—OK, a rock band—or a major airport similar to JFK in New York or O'Hare in Chicago. The orchestra and the airport have many things in common. For our purposes, we look at the fact that, in order for them to work properly, everything has to come together at exactly the right time. Otherwise, there is chaos. Passengers would be stranded all over the place, or music lovers would walk out of the concert because the quality of the musical performance is unpleasant. Your body can be thought of as that large orchestra or airport. There are many different parts to you and they must all play in harmony to get a pleasant effect. With the airport and the orchestra, there is also a conductor or controller making sure that it all works. Your brain is that conductor. Your brain controls your thoughts, your behavior, your physical functions, and your ability to connect with other people. Your brain sends messages to the rest of your body and other parts of your brain and tells them what to do. You are reading this book because your brain is sending signals to your hand to turn the pages and to your eyes to see the words and to other parts of the brain that help you understand what you are seeing.

In this chapter, you will get a better understanding of how your brain works like it does and why it may work differently from the brains of your friends who don't seem to have any problems in school or in their social lives. Scientists have new tools that are able to look at people's brains doing an activity and tell what the brain is doing while this activity is going on. This research is somewhat new and is changing what we know about how our brain works. The information you read today may change tomorrow, so only the basics will be included here. Scientists are hoping that information gathered with these new tools will eventually lead to new treatments and interventions that will help people with learning disabilities.

How Your Brain Works

Your brain is still growing and changing. Researchers used to think that a brain was fully developed by the time a person was three years old. Studies have shown that is not true. Parts of your brain continue to change throughout your life. During the teen years, the number of cells expands and some of them, ones you no longer use, wither away. The good news is, according to Dr. Jay Giedd of the National Institute of Mental Health in Bethesda, Maryland, the cells you need for important tasks normally survive, and there is actually a huge growth spurt around the time of puberty. Dr. Giedd's study showed that the white matter of the brain (the part that connects the different parts of the brain) grows steadily. The gray matter (the part that controls your processing and thinking) has a growth spurt in the teenage years. This is more good news because it gives you a second chance to tighten the circuitry of your brain by stretching yourself and trying to use as many parts as possible to make sure they are not lost. The brain cells that are used get more nutrients and that helps them survive. The choices you make determine which connections survive and which don't. Dr. John Ratey, author of *A User's Guide to the Brain*, recommends a "use it or lose it" strategy when it comes to strengthening brain connections. Although it is often a struggle to learn new things, the learning process strengthens the brain.

> While a brain may be weak in one area, it likely has a corresponding strength in another.... Each brain is different, and each is more efficient at certain kinds of processing than others.
>
> —John A. Ratey, M.D.
> *A User's Guide to the Brain*

Researchers have proven activity improves brain function, and they also know that poor choices can do permanent harm. The abuse of drugs and alcohol can damage the brain by destroying the outer lining of nerve cells and interfering with their ability to communicate.

It is hard to believe that the brain weighs only three pounds. It looks like a gray, unshelled walnut. It is the most complex structure in our world and your body's most vital organ. At birth, your brain has over 100 billion cells (neurons). These cells signal to thousands of other cells in the body at speeds of more than 200 miles an hour. Your brain has three major parts—the cerebrum, the cerebellum, and the brain stem. Since this is not a test, you don't need to remember the names, but it is important to understand what each part does.

The Cerebral Hemisphere

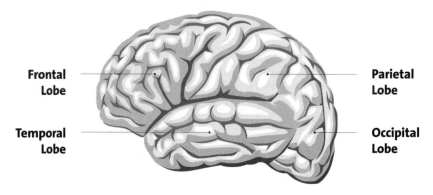

Frontal
Lobe

Parietal
Lobe

Temporal
Lobe

Occipital
Lobe

Figure 2.1
The brain is divided into halves called hemispheres. Each hemisphere is divided into four sections, or lobes: the frontal, the parietal, the temporal, and the occipital.

The Cerebrum

The brain, also known as the cerebrum, is made up of the frontal lobe, the parietal lobe, the temporal lobe, and the occipital lobe, and is divided into two hemispheres. It also contains the corpus callosum, the basal ganglia, and the limbic system.

The hemispheres. The cerebrum is divided into hemispheres. In most people, the left hemisphere is dominant. The left hemisphere usually controls the right side of the body and controls language, mathematics, abstraction, reasoning, and cognitive functions. The left hemisphere interprets information systematically and logically and stores memory in a language format.

The right hemisphere controls the left side of the body and is in charge of nonverbal processes such as attention, pattern recognition, line orientation, and the detection of complex sounds. The right side helps you integrate information to get a complete picture of your

Hemispheres

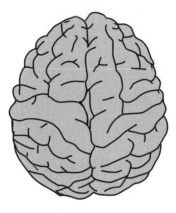

Figure 2.2
The longitudinal fissure divides the brain into two halves, called hemispheres.

environment. Information processed on the right side is more visual-spatial and has to do with how you see yourself within a space. This side coordinates activities such as dancing and gymnastics. Memory in the right hemisphere is stored in auditory, visual, and spatial formats rather than language formats. There is more white matter in the right side of the brain. The white matter is the highway system that connects the information centers of the brain and allows information to be processed accurately. Because those with nonverbal learning disabilities have difficulty processing and making sense of information, some believe that NLD is caused by damage to this highway and call it a right hemisphere disability.

Although each hemisphere acts independently, the two hemispheres are in continual communication.

The corpus callosum. The corpus callosum connects right and left hemispheres to allow for communication between the two sides.

Girls have more connectors and these connectors help them utilize both sides of the brain during language functions. This may explain why boys have more trouble compensating for dyslexia than girls.

The frontal lobe. The frontal lobe takes longer to mature than the other parts of the brain. It might not become efficient until age sixteen and doesn't reach maturity until you are between eighteen and twenty. This section of the brain determines your personality and emotions. It controls judgment, organization, impulses, sexual behavior, language, and movement. It allows you to plan difficult tasks, to control emotions, and to inhibit inappropriate behavior. This is the part of the brain that makes you stop and think. If attention and organization are difficult for you, researchers now believe it is probably due to a problem in the frontal lobe. Since you still have a few years before your twentieth birthday, your attention problems may improve as your frontal lobe matures.

There are two frontal lobes (left and right) and each lobe has two parts. The front is called the prefrontal cortex. It is where the higher cognitive functions are located and where executive decisions are made. This part of your brain determines your personality and is responsible for who you are as an individual. The back contains the premotor and motor areas that control and produce movement.

The parietal lobe. The parietal lobe reaches its peak during the teen years. It controls how we understand and process information about the environment and helps us understand what we see and feel. This lobe integrates information from other areas of the brain, so difficulties in understanding how things relate to each other may originate in this area. This parietal lobe is also made up of parts. The primary sensory cortex is the part that controls sensation (touch, pressure). Behind the primary sensory cortex is a large area that controls fine sensation (judgment of texture, weight, size, and shape). A left side and a right side also define the parietal lobe. The left side deals with your ability to understand language. The right side helps you understand your world in space. This side helps you find your way around new and familiar places. Differences in this part of the brain may be involved in nonverbal learning disabilities.

The temporal lobe.   The temporal lobe reaches its maximum development at age sixteen. It controls hearing and the ability to recognize words and is involved with short- and long-term memory. It is the seat of language and emotional control and gives words to your world. Because of the heavy involvement with language, it gives interpretation and meaning to incoming information. There are two temporal lobes. The right lobe is involved with visual memory—pictures, faces, and so forth. The left lobe deals with verbal memory—words and name. When you meet someone new, and you can remember a person's name and not the face, it may be that you are working with the left temporal lobe. If you can remember the person's face but not the name, it may be you are working with the right temporal lobe. Problems on one side may contribute to problems with language, while problems on the other side may contribute to nonverbal learning disabilities.

The occipital lobe.   The occipital lobe is the center where vision is processed. It helps us understand what we are looking at and helps us identify shapes and colors.

The basal ganglia.   The basal ganglion forms the processing center located deep inside the brain. It integrates your feelings and movements. If you jump as a reflex when you are excited, it is probably because of the basal ganglia. Balance and postural reflexes are located here.

The limbic system.   The limbic system is in the center of the brain and influences unconscious, instinctive behaviors. It plays a role in the expression of your emotions, your motivation, your sense of smell, your pleasure and pain centers, your sleep, and your appetite. This system allows you to connect with people and have relationships. It sounds like it has many of the same functions as the frontal lobes, but it acts more primitively than the frontal lobes.

The Brain Stem

The brain stem controls breathing, heart rate, blood pressure, and digestion. It connects the spinal cord to the brain and controls the functions that keep you alive.

The Cerebellum

The cerebellum is located at the base of the back of the brain and controls balance, coordination, and movement. When you turn the pages of this book, it is your cerebellum at work without your being aware of it.

Inside the Brain

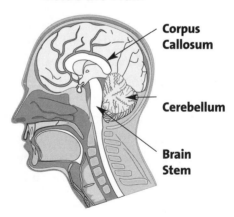

Figure 2.3
This image of the brain shows the corpus callosum, which consists of millions of nerve fibers and connects the two hemispheres of the cerebrum. The brain stem links the brain to the spinal cord. The cerebellum is in back of the brain and helps us coordinate our movements and maintain balance.

Neurons

All of these parts of the brain need to communicate with each other and that is done by way of the neurons or nerve cells. Neurons are made up of nerve cell bodies, dendrites, and axons. They are different from other cells in that they can receive and send signals to other neurons. They power the process that turns thoughts into actions by sending signals to another cell with the help of neurotransmitters, chemicals that are sent between the cells. These neurotransmitters jump across the synaptic gap (a distance much smaller than a thousandth of a millimeter) to be picked up by the receptors on the ends

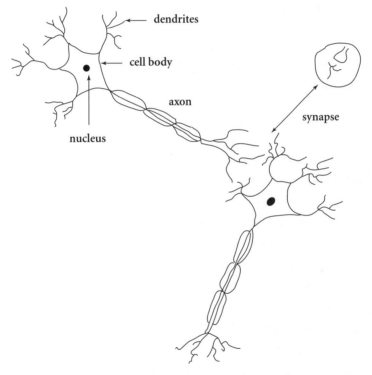

Figure 2.4
Dendrites reach out and pick up signals from other cells. Axons send the outgoing signal from the neuron. The place of contact between the axon of one cell and a dendrite of another is called a synapse.

of the dendrites of a neighboring neuron. The neurotransmitter is absorbed by the new cell and the cell changes in response.

The dendrites branch out from the cell body like unruly hair. They can be thought of as electrical cables bringing the signal from another cell. The axon sends the outgoing signal from the neuron. The place of contact between the axon of one cell and a dendrite of another is called a synapse. The signals jump from cell to cell until they get to the part of the body that acts. If the neurotransmitters are not working properly, the messages will not get to where they need to go, or they will get there too slowly to make for efficiency.

Current Technology and Research

Scientists and researchers continue to examine the brain to determine its role in specific learning disabilities. New technological tools and tests are helping them develop theories related to learning.

fMRI

One of the new technologies allowing researchers to explore the brain is functional Magnetic Resonance Imaging (fMRI). fMRI can sense the changes in the natural magnetic properties of blood cells that carry oxygen. Active, stimulated brain cells need more oxygen, and an increased blood flow to the area provides that oxygen. fMRI can capture pictures of this increased blood flow because oxygen-rich cells send different signals than oxygen-depleted cells. This allows researchers not only to see pictures of the brain, but also to observe how the brain works during specific activities. With this new technology, researchers can *see* how the brains of those with ADHD respond differently to a particular activity than those without the disorder, for example.

In order to get an fMRI brain image, the patient's head is placed within a large, cylindrical magnet that creates a strong magnetic field.

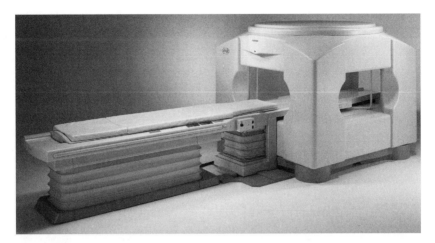

Figure 2.5
The Toshiba OPART MRI technology. Photo provided by Toshiba America Medical Systems, Inc.

Then radio waves are sent through the field and sensors read the signals. A computer then processes the data and provides colorful images recording the brain's activity. The most active areas show up red.

PET

No, researchers aren't using puppies, kittens, or goldfish to measure brain activity, but a method called Positron Emission Tomography (PET). PET measures activities from radioactively enhanced chemicals that are injected into the bloodstream. Researchers inject a form of sugar into the bloodstream, along with small amounts of a radioactive tracer, and then make photographs of the brain and brain activity. The images record biochemical changes in the brain. PET can show blood flow, oxygen and glucose metabolism, and drug concentrations in the tissues of the brain. It can be used to identify the brain sites where drugs and neurotransmitters act and show how quickly drugs reach and activate neural receptors, how long they stay there, and how long it takes for them to leave the brain.

Computers are used to process the information and to create two- or three-dimensional images of chemicals in the brain.

SPECT

The Single Photon Emission Computed Tomography (SPECT) is similar to PET because it also uses radioactive tracers and a scanner to record the data, and computers to process and create the images. It is more limited than PET in the kinds of brain activity it can monitor, but because the equipment is less expensive and requires less specialized

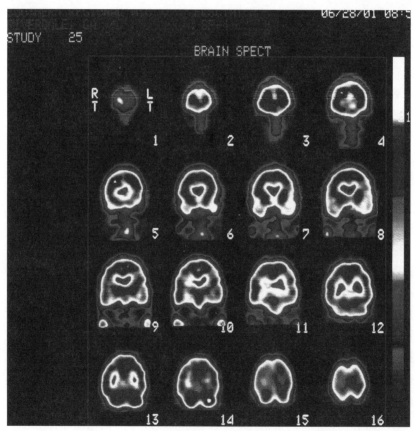

SPECT scans are helping researchers understand the brain chemistry involved in learning disabilities.

equipment and staff support, it is more readily available. It is being used to answer some of the same questions about brain chemistry

These new technologies are being used to research learning disabilities and are providing clues to differences in the brains of those with and without the disorders.

How the Brain Affects Learning

Are you still with us?

Now, you might wonder, how does all of this tie into learning? Though the brain can be broken down into specific areas, all of your brain functions need to be coordinated, integrated, and synchronized in order for learning to take place. If not, we need to find out where the breakdown is occurring in order to help you learn.

According to Dr. Mel Levine in his book *All Kinds of Minds*, you need to be able to do the following in order to learn:

* You need to be able to concentrate and focus on one thing rather than another, finish a task, and control what you say and do.
* You need to be able to understand time and sequence of events.
* You need to be able to tell the differences between different images.
* You need to be able to store and recall information.
* You need to be able to understand and express language.
* You need to be able to coordinate motor and muscle movements.
* You need to be able to make friends and work in groups.
* You need to be able to solve problems and think creatively.
* And you need to be able to do all these things at the same time.

Now try to imagine your brain as an air traffic controller keeping many planes in the air at the same time, allowing one plane to land and another to take off without crashing into each other. That is what your brain is doing every time you are trying to complete your schoolwork. If you have a learning disability in a specific area, differences in the structure of your brain and the coordination of activities in your brain may create problems with learning.

ADHD

In 1998, researchers at Stanford University reported results of an fMRI study indicating that there is a biological marker for ADHD. The study measured the brain activity of young people with ADHD while they were taking the stimulant medication Ritalin and again while they were not taking the drug. They also measured the brain activities of children without ADHD. In some parts of the test measuring impulsivity, children with ADHD (while not taking drugs) had measurable differences in brain activity from those without ADHD. When both groups took the drug, brain activities increased for both groups during some tests, but during other tests brain activities differed between the two groups. Researchers believe this type of study confirms brain differences in those with ADHD compared to those without ADHD and may provide a biological tool for diagnosing the disorder.

Also in 1998, researchers at Massachusetts General Hospital in Boston reported biochemical differences in people with ADHD. They used brain scans to measure the movement of chemicals in the brain. A brain chemical called dopamine is transferred from one cell to another through neural networks in the brain. This chemical has been associated with movement, thought, motivation, and pleasure—the very tasks involved in executive functions. Those with ADHD had 70 percent more dopamine transporters than those without the disorder. Those with ADHD appear to have problems with the transfer of dopamine between the senders or transporters of the chemical and receivers or receptors of the chemical. At this time, scientists are unsure whether the problem is caused by too much or too little dopamine. Other research has shown a clear-cut chemical abnormality in the part of the brain that uses the dopamine. They are hoping that this finding will lead them to a medical test to diagnose the disorder. If a test can be developed, it will help with decisions about treatment.

Several studies have found additional information about the brain and ADHD. In some studies, the areas that regulate attention have been found to be smaller in some people with ADHD. Other research has shown that the neurons in the frontal lobe are not firing efficiently. The brain areas that control attention appear to be more active in those with ADHD, perhaps indicating that those with ADHD must work harder to control their impulses.

If you have ADHD, it may be difficult for you to do what you need to do because you have difficulty with concentration and focus. These recent studies provide evidence that this is caused by differences within the brain, not because you are "lazy" or a "spaceshot" or a "daydreamer," but because your brain operates differently.

As research continues, we will learn more about ADHD and the effects of stimulant medications. In the meantime, read the ADHD chapter (chapter 3) to get a better understanding of the disorder and to pick up some tips that may help you in school.

Dyslexia

With dyslexia, studies show differences in the structure and functioning of the brain. There is more than one type of reading disability so there is more than one reason for the disability. More than one area of the brain may be involved in any one person's disability. A language-related area found on both sides of the brain is the same size in some people with dyslexia; in those without dyslexia, the left side is usually larger.

If the problem is a working memory problem, several areas of the brain may be involved. If it is a problem recognizing and sequencing sounds that occur too close together, the cause may be located in another area of the brain. If the problem is related to the rapid processing of information, the cause could be somewhere else entirely. Because of the complexity of a reading disability and the intricacy of the brain, it is not currently possible to point to a particular brain malformation for the cause of dyslexia. However, researchers continue to try to look at brain images and try to pinpoint problem areas. Current research can explain some of the problems but its origins continue to be an ongoing mystery.

Drs. Sally and Bennett Shaywitz, codirectors of the Yale University Center for the Study of Learning and Attention Disorders, have discovered through brain images that good readers use both the front and back of the brain for phonological processing tasks. Those with dyslexia show overactivity in the front area of the brain, and no activity in the back. These researchers believe this is the brain's way of trying to compensate for the deficits in other areas of the brain. The brain is actually stimulating different areas in an effort to process written language in an alternative way. Dr. Sally Shaywitz explains, "These brain activation patterns now provide us with hard evidence of a disruption in the brain regions responsible for reading—evidence for what has previously been a hidden disability."

Researcher Barry Horwitz and his colleagues at the National Institutes of Health (NIH) used PET to examine blood flow in various regions of the brain as men with dyslexia and those without the disorder were in the process of reading. In readers without disabilities, several regions of the brain worked during the reading process. Those with dyslexia show a lack of communication between the regions of the brain believed to be involved in reading. Their findings suggest a "disconnection" of the part of the brain thought to play a critical role in relating letters to speech from the occipital and temporal lobes, brain areas involved in visual and language processing.

It should make you feel a little better that part of the problem appears to be the complexity of our language. English has a more puzzling and complex way of putting sounds together to form words. Therefore, it might be harder for you to hear the sounds of the English language. Other languages, particularly Italian in a recent study, are shown to have only one way to represent a sound. Even Italian-speaking people have dyslexia, but it doesn't cause as many problems for them in school because the sounds of the language are easier to work with.

Research now helps us explain why some people have a harder time with written and spoken language than others. As research continues to find new possibilities, there may be improvements in both the diagnosis and the strategies used to help those with language and reading disorders.

Math

Dr. David Geary, a psychologist and specialist in mathematical disabilities, believes that different types of math learning problems involve different areas of the brain. Some of them are caused by problems with semantic memory (see below). He believes students who have trouble with procedural tasks and those with semantic memory problems may have problems located in the left hemisphere of the brain. Those with visual-spatial problems in math are having right hemisphere dysfunction, particularly the posterior regions.

Nonverbal Learning Disabilities

With nonverbal learning disabilities (NLD), the cause or causes are still under investigation. NLD is a right-hemisphere syndrome characterized by deficits in nonverbal reasoning. Brain scans of those with NLD often show differences in the right hemisphere. This right side is the area of the brain that can work with both visual and verbal information at the same time. As a result, it can help us read a person's facial expressions and gestures and combine that information with what a person is saying to get a clear understanding of not only what the person says, but also what the person means as well. This is the kind of skill that gives those with NLD so much trouble.

According to NLD specialist Dr. Byron Rourke, there are indications that the white matter of the brain is involved in this type of disability. There may be damage to the long myelinated fibers in the brain that help make the important connections necessary in helping the right side of the brain operate smoothly. The left side of the brain—the side that handles information in a step-by-step way, controls speech, and is useful in skills such as memorization—is not affected. As a result, those with NLD rely on left-brain ways of learning.

Differences in the corpus callosum may also be involved. This collection of millions of nerves is located between the two sides of the brain. They help the two sides work together. If there is under-development in or damage to this area, the left and right sides of the brain have difficulty working together. Sometimes, the differences in the brain have been caused by specific damage as a result of injury, tumors, radiation, and/or seizures. Still, there is no indication that everyone affected by NLD has suffered a brain injury

Memory

Storage and recall of information is an important function of the brain and it is a crucial function in any kind of learning. Even the best student in the class forgets things sometimes. It is important to know how your brain works in order to come up with ways to improve your memory so you can recall the information you need in order to work out a problem in class or to pass a test. Your brain receives information from the outside world through eyes, ears, nose, skin, or movement. That information is held from one to two seconds while the brain decides whether to keep it, store it, or discard it. This is the area of short-term memory and the information gets there through your attention to it. It is what allows you to remember the beginning of this sentence until you get to the end so you will understand it. It is also what allows you to remember your friend's phone number after you looked it up, long enough to dial it.

If the information is kept, it goes to the area of working memory. Your working memory allows you to hold several thoughts temporarily while you solve a problem. It is what allows you to do a math problem in your head. You have to hold onto more than one chunk of information and use the information to do something, like solve that math problem or follow the three directions your chemistry teacher gave you. It is the transfer station between short-term memory and long-term memory. Difficulties in the area of working memory affect all areas of your schoolwork. You need a good working memory in order to make sense of just about everything in school. It helps you remember and understand what you hear and what you read, to allow you to write sentences and paragraphs on a topic, to do problem-solving tasks, and to perform math operations. Once information is in working memory, you use it to complete a task or it gets stored in long-term memory.

If the information is stored in long-term memory, it can be recalled for later use. If information is stored in your long-term memory efficiently, it makes it easier for you to recall it to solve those math problems. If you have memorized your multiplication facts and have them stored in an organized way in your long-term memory, you will be able to use those facts while working with fractions.

There are several other types of memory as well. With procedural memory or motor memory, you learn by doing. This is what you use when you learn how to ride a bicycle or perform a gymnastics move. Reflexive memory is an automatic reaction that you use when you are recalling information you know really well. Semantic memory is based on words. It uses associations to help with the storage and retrieval of facts. Episodic memory is what you use to write the essay on the first day of school about what you did on your summer vacation. This type of memory is based on experience and events, which are much easier to remember than those math facts.

Memory is scattered through many areas of the brain, not just one area. There must be organization between the different areas of the brain in order for you to remember information. You can improve your memory by knowing how your brain works and by knowing which senses are stronger and better able to receive and process information. If you learn better by seeing something, you will remember what you see better than what you hear. If you learn best through touch, you will need to do something with your hands in order to commit it to memory. Reading about taking an engine apart will not stick with you as long as it would if you were actually taking the engine apart and putting it back together again.

You use your memory constantly to help yourself recall information and use it in school, at home, at work, and socially. And, as you might guess, there is more than one kind of information retrieval. The type of retrieval you use in order to answer essay questions is recall. The information comes directly from your memory and you can find it and use it whenever you need it. Recognition memory is what you use for answering multiple-choice questions. The information is remembered when you are given a cue or hint about it. You may have difficulty knowing the correct answer if someone asked you who invented the telephone, but if you were given a choice of Albert Einstein, Alexander Graham Bell, or Thomas Edison, you would probably remember that it was Bell.

These differences in types of memory can be seen during specific tasks using fMRI scans.

An understanding of the brain and of recent research findings can help you better understand why you learn the way that you do.

Attention Deficit Hyperactivity Disorder

How It Feels to Have ADHD

When students with Attention Deficit Hyperactivity Disorder (ADHD) talk about what it is like to deal with the issue, they often say they feel like a giant motor is driving them and they have trouble controlling its power, its direction, and its speed. As the Joey Pigza character says in Jack Gantos's novel *Joey Pigza Swallowed the Key*, "There's no doubt about it, I'm wired."

Not all students have the hyperactive symptoms Joey describes. Some have problems in the other areas associated with ADHD. Some, like guitarist Jon Finn, have organizational problems.

Other young people say they just can't concentrate or they find themselves daydreaming or they blurt out things they really didn't mean to say aloud. Some have a hard time sitting still in class. Others are thrill seekers, looking for exciting things to do. Do these things sound familiar? Why do people behave that way anyway?

A Definition

ADHD is neurobiological disorder that includes a combination of inattentive, hyperactive, and impulsive behaviors that are developmentally inappropriate and severe

At school they say I'm wired bad, or wired mad, or wired sad, or wired glad, depending on my mood and what teacher has ended up with me. But there is no doubt about it. I'm *wired*.

—Joey Pigza
Joey Pigza Swallowed the Key
by Jack Gantos

The day I decided to get help was when I completely forgot to show up at a gig. There was no excuse or reason. The date was marked in my datebook. I had spent several hours in the preceding days preparing for it. When the day came, I had no sense whatsoever that I was supposed to be somewhere.

—Jon Finn, guitarist and rock guitar teacher

enough to impair function at home and school. What that mouthful means is that this disorder is brain-based (not caused by your parents, or your teachers, or your desire to disrupt). It may cause you to behave in ways that keep you from performing the way you would like to in school, in your activities, and even in social situations. ADHD is the most commonly diagnosed behavioral disorder of childhood. If you have ADHD, your symptoms may include the inability to pay attention, problems concentrating, hyperactivity, distractibility, and/or impulsivity. Although ADHD is classified as a behavioral disorder, not a learning disability, we include it because it is a disorder that affects learning. According to the National Institutes of Health (NIH), between 3 and 5 percent of school-age children have ADHD, and a recent article in *Scientific American* claims that as many as 9.5 percent of school-age children worldwide have ADHD. You are not alone.

There are three types of ADHD: the predominantly inattentive type, the predominantly hyperactive-impulsive type, and a combined type; as you might expect, there are three types of symptoms. Right now, symptoms and behaviors are used to diagnose ADHD. Criteria are established for diagnosing the disorder in a book called *The Diagnostic and Statistical Manual of Mental Disorders* (DSM-IV). According to this resource book used by physicians when diagnosing disorders, those diagnosed with ADHD must have six or more of these symptoms in each category for more than six months. If you have ADHD, you exhibit many of the following symptoms:

Inattention

✳ You fail to give close attention to details or make careless mistakes.

✳ You have trouble paying attention during tasks or activities.

✳ You don't seem to listen when spoken to.

✳ You have trouble following instructions and often fail to complete tasks (including homework and chores).

☀ You have organizational problems.

☀ You avoid or dislike tasks that require sustained mental effort (like homework).

☀ You often lose things (your homework, your book report, your car keys).

☀ You are easily distracted.

☀ You are forgetful.

Hyperactive Behaviors

☀ You fidget. You can't keep your hands or feet still, or you squirm in your seat.

☀ You leave your seat when you shouldn't.

☀ You often feel restless.

☀ You have trouble engaging in leisure activities quietly.

☀ You are often "on the go," always in motion.

☀ You talk a lot.

Impulsive Behaviors

☀ You speak or act without taking the time to think—you blurt out answers.

☀ You interrupt or intrude on others.

☀ You have trouble waiting and are generally impatient.

Research shows that boys are diagnosed with ADHD more than girls are, but recent findings indicate that may be because boys display more of the disruptive symptoms, calling attention to themselves and their problems. Girls are more likely to have the inattentive form of this disorder and their problems are sometimes overlooked or misdiagnosed as laziness. ADHD can present problems in many areas of learning.

Executive Function: What It Is and How It Is Related to ADHD

The term *executive function* may make you think of corporate meetings, or CEOs, or business reports, but when discussing ADHD, executive functions have more to do with how you apply the information you have. You may hear this term used during discussions of ADHD, and it is important to know how the term relates to ADHD.

The thought processes that help you plan, set goals, carry out your plans, and control your behavior may be affected if you have ADHD. These tasks are called executive functions. Problems in this area may include the inability to:

* Make plans
* Set goals
* Organize and carry out the plans necessary to reach goals
* Solve problems
* Follow rules
* Remember and learn from past experience
* Learn and obey social conventions
* Place incidents in time and place

As might be expected, if you have ADHD and the related problems with executive functions, you probably act more often on impulse rather than taking the time to think things through.

Dr. Russell Barkley, a psychiatrist at the University of Massachusetts Medical Center, has spent years researching the effects of executive function deficits on young people. He believes these tasks can be broken down into four categories:

* Working memory
* Self-regulation or internalized emotion
* Internalized speech
* Reconstitution or inventiveness

Working Memory

Working memory involves the ability to remember events or information long enough to use that information again when making new decisions, solving problems, or performing a task. Problems with working memory can be responsible for reading problems, math problems, and social problems. You need to hold onto things that you have learned, not only to pass a test but also to help you create a plan for your future or to set goals. Teenagers with ADHD often have problems in this area, making it hard to put the steps needed for success in the right order. It you can't predict the consequences of an action based on previous experience, you may have trouble remembering the things that got you into trouble in the first place. If what happened in the past was a result of a bad decision, you may not remember past actions well enough to avoid another mistake. Decisions that helped you succeed in the past may also be lost in the maze of working memory. If you can't recall past successes, you can't use that information again to assure success in the future. For those with working memory issues, it is hard to get excited about something that will happen in the future and to carry out the steps necessary to make that happen again. Because of these problems, working memory deficits can affect your ability, and as a consequence, your desire, to set goals.

Self-Regulation

Self-regulation involves the ability to control emotions—the ability to keep quiet when you would like to yell at someone, the ability to hold back when what you really want to do is slam a door, the ability to keep your hands under control when you really want to punch a wall. Deficits with this self-control can create major issues at school, at home, and sometimes even with the law. Problems in this area can also be distracting. It is hard to keep goals in mind when emotions get in the way.

Internalized Speech

Young children often talk to themselves. They may talk themselves through the steps necessary to perform a task. As we get older, we still talk to ourselves, but we do it silently, in our minds. This is called internalized speech. We use this self-talk to tell ourselves how to accomplish a task, how to behave, and how not to behave. If you don't talk to yourself before you act, you may have behavior problems, social skills problems, and problems accomplishing what you set out to do.

Reconstitution or Inventiveness

Reconstitution is the ability to break things down that we have learned in the past and then reorder them in a way that helps us create new ideas. Dr. Barry Skoff of North Shore Children's Hospital in Massachusetts recommends thinking of the brain as a "filing cabinet." Those with trouble organizing information will have trouble finding the information that has been filed away. Because those with ADHD tend to search for information randomly rather than systematically, the results of searching will vary widely. Sometimes the information will be right in the front of the file, easy to find and use. At other times, the necessary facts or thoughts are buried away and are seemingly impossible to find. If you can't find the information, you won't be able to use it. But, as important, if you are unable to learn a systematic way of filing and retrieving information, you won't have a method you can rely on for searching.

Together these *executive functions* help you plan for the future and maintain self-control. These skills become more essential as you get older. The type of work required in high school and in college needs more organization and planning, and teenagers are expected to work independently. The good news is that these four tasks are controlled in the prefrontal cortex (see chapter 2) and that part of the brain continues to develop into the late teens. If you are having problems in these areas, they may improve over the next couple of years. However, these problems often continue into adulthood, and coping strategies are essential if you are to set and achieve goals.

The executive function problems associated with ADHD create problems for many teenagers. Those who have ADHD and have survived their high school years and learned to cope and often to flourish despite the disability have a lot to say about the effects of ADHD and the impact it has on their lives. See more about this in the Good News section below.

Brief Overview of Possible Causes

As with most learning disabilities, it is still impossible to pinpoint the exact cause of ADHD. Brain imaging studies, however, are beginning to provide visible evidence of differences in the brains of those with ADHD. Recent research by the National Institute of Mental Health reveals that portions of the brains of children with ADHD are smaller than those who do not have the disorder. Now don't go thinking that because portions of your brain might be smaller that you are less intelligent. These areas of the brain do not regulate intelligence but, as might be expected, they regulate attention, they may help control behaviors, and they may play a role in regulating motivation.

The brain areas that control attention appear to be less active in those with ADHD, perhaps indicating that those with ADHD must work harder to control their impulses. You can read more about the brain and the recent studies in chapter 2.

Most evidence indicates that genetics plays a role in up to 80 percent of ADHD cases and that the disorder is probably inherited. Researchers have found that those with a parent or a sibling with ADHD are more likely to have the disorder. Studies of identical twins have confirmed the likelihood that ADHD is inherited.

Premature birth, maternal alcohol use and abuse, exposure to lead in early childhood, and brain injuries may also play a role in 20 to 30 percent of the other cases.

Causes of ADHD will continue to be under investigation for years to come. In the meantime, you should know that your personality, your temperament, and your other strengths play a role in your ability to maintain the self-control so necessary for success in school and in life.

Treatment Options and Coping Strategies

If ADHD is preventing you from being successful in school, at home, or in social settings, your doctor may recommend treating you with a stimulant medication such as methylphenidate (Ritalin) or amphetamines (Dexedrine, Dextrostat, and Aderall) to decrease impulsivity and hyperactivity and to improve attention. Benefits of these medications, once thought just appropriate for younger children, are now routinely prescribed for adolescents and young adults as well. Newer, longer-acting medications, such as Concerta, may be recommended for older children and young adults. A doctor must prescribe any treatment with medications. If you are not already on medications, you may want to discuss this option with your parents and your doctor.

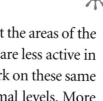

> When I take Ritalin I can still hear the voices outside the classroom, but I can ignore them.
>
> —Paul, high school student

Information provided from the National Institutes of Health explains the puzzle of prescribing a stimulant for hyperactivity. Researchers there say that the areas of the brain thought to be involved in executive functions are less active in persons with ADHD. Stimulant medication may work on these same areas of the brain, increasing activity to more normal levels. More research, however, is needed to confirm this theory. This type of treatment may manage symptoms well enough for those with ADHD to learn academic and social strategies that improve their lives.

Side effects may include loss of appetite and problems with sleep, but these usually diminish over time or can be lessened with adjustments in doses. The length of treatment with stimulant medications varies. Side effects and changes in dosages must be discussed with your doctor.

The use of stimulant medication is a controversial one. Debate rages over the appropriateness of drug treatment for ADHD, and many believe it is overprescribed. When research improves the diagnostic methods used for the disorder and provides additional information on the use of stimulant medications, the answers may become clearer. Researchers are now looking for a nonstimulant medication to help with the disorder. Until then, the decision to use medications should be made by you, your parents, and a physician with a solid background in treating young people with ADHD.

If together you decide to take a medicinal approach to help treat ADHD, be sure you know what you are taking and how it affects you. Special education teachers and disabilities services coordinators at colleges that we spoke to said students often don't know what they are taking or what they should expect from the drugs. If you are getting ready to leave for college, be sure you know what you are taking and the recommended dosage. Be sure to let the medical professionals at your school know you are taking medications. They can help you if you have questions or problems.

Some students decide that their first year in college is the time to try to come off medications. Specialist we talked to advised against that.

Many young people also find counseling helpful, along with or without stimulant medications. Counseling can provide coping strategies to help deal with ADHD, and is often helpful in improving social interactions.

Many students take advantage of special education programs and counseling at their schools to learn the strategies necessary for success. Professionals who work with students who have ADHD and those who have learned to compensate for ADHD symptoms often make the same recommendations. If you are working with special educators in high school, or if you are using the services provided at your college, you can benefit from many of the strategies provided there. It is important to get more than help in memorizing work for tests. The most important lessons you can learn involve strategies that you can use over and over again. Here are recommendations we have collected from a variety of sources:

Write Things Down

You may think you are the only one who needs to write things down to remember them. In fact, most people use lists of some kind to organize their lives. Since memory can be an issue, help yourself out by giving yourself a written reminder of what needs to be done. Not only does it act as a visual cue, but also the very act of writing things down improves your chances of remembering.

Keep a Journal or a Diary

For those who have problems with self-talk, writing thoughts in a journal can help them slow down and think before acting. It can help as an organizational tool and as a place to sort through your thoughts and emotions.

Use an Assignment Notebook

Most students know they should do that, but often they forget to look at it. Set aside a particular time each day to review your assignments. Put a reminder on your computer, put a sticky note on your VCR, on your audio equipment, or on your phone (or any other object you use regularly). Check off your assignments as you complete them. This little activity can give an enormous sense of accomplishment, especially when the assignment was a difficult one.

Use a Calendar, Day Planner, or Organizer

As you get older, you become involved in more and more activities. Keeping it all straight is an enormous challenge. Help yourself; write down your activities. Make notes that include long-term assignments. That way you will know if you have school-related work that must be done and won't schedule an activity that might distract you from doing your work the very weekend you are expected to write a term paper.

Use Your Computer

If you use your computer every day, you can keep a calendar or day-planner there. There are even software programs that will give you a reminder if you need one. Send yourself an e-mail reminder, or ask a friend to send you one.

Your computer can also be used as a backup system. Often students work hard to complete projects and then lose them. Remember to save your work on your computer. Save it on your hard drive and save it on a disk. When you print it, make two copies. Take one with you and leave one at home. If you don't have a computer, always make a photocopy of your reports and projects.

Get Organized

There are a variety of organizational tricks you can use to help you keep your work where you can find it. High school and college students often struggle to complete projects and then can't find them when it is time to turn them in. Recognize that this may be a problem for you and take control. Though "a place for everything and everything in its place" may seem like a trite expression, it may be the only way you can manage. Choose one place to keep your schoolwork and *always* put it there.

Backpacks

Most students keep schoolwork in a backpack. To an outsider, these often look like a portable trash bin. If you can find things in your backpack, fine. If not, get some colored folders (those with pockets that keep papers from falling out). Put the work for each class in a different colored folder. Because your brain has trouble with organization, give it an assist. You will be able to find you work more easily if it is organized.

Your Room

Many teenagers thrive in what appears to be chaos. Littered rooms are not unusual, but you can't afford that kind of mess. At least set aside one area of your room where you can find what you are looking for.

Organize Your Time

With all there is to do, this is one of the most important skills you can work on. For most teenagers, keeping a time log can be a revelation. Make a list of all of the things you do outside of school and how much time you spend on them each day. At the end of the week take a look at exactly how much time you are spending with friends, watching television, doing homework, and so on. Most young people are surprised by how little time they actually spend on school-related activities. Look for activities that are taking necessary hours away from school assignments and begin cutting back those activities to allow more time for assignments.

Calendars, day planners, and assignment books can all help you get a visual overview of what you have to do. Computers will give you reminders. There are watches complete with alarms, buzzers, or blinking lights that can be set to give you a gentle nudge. Timers not only provide structure for your work time but they can be set to give you break time, too.

One of the most effective ways to handle long-term assignments or big projects is to break them down into smaller assignments. Create a plan of attack by dividing the job into manageable pieces. Do them one at a time and be sure to check them off a checklist as you finish.

Procrastination is a problem for everyone. Sometimes it is just so hard to get started. That's okay. Allow yourself some time to procrastinate, but limit that time. Set a timer and listen to CDs, call a friend, or watch television for a half hour. But, at the end of the half hour, when the timer goes off, you must get to work.

Work at your best time. Some people work best in the morning. There are also night owls who don't hit their strides until the moon is high. When you work at your best times of the day, you get your best work done in the shortest period of time. Think about your best time and try to schedule your schoolwork for that time of day. If you are an early bird, get up an hour earlier and do your assignment then. If you would rather work at night, that's fine, too. One warning, however: most teenagers don't get enough sleep. If you work past midnight, you are going to have a hard time getting up in the morning. Even if you do get up, you will be working at a sleep-deprived disadvantage all day. Try to get enough sleep!

Set Priorities

Take a realistic look at your calendar and prioritize your activities. Put a number next to each activity and assignment on your calendar. Mark the most important ones with a number 1, moderately important with a 2, least important with a 3. Each day, tackle the ones first. Do the twos next. If you have time, do the threes. If your goal is to improve your grade in science, science assignments always get a one. You can't give all of your other assignments threes each day, however. This method not only helps you set priorities, but it helps break down your activities and work into manageable portions.

Stay Focused in the Classroom

Since you spend a great deal of time in school and since that may create the biggest challenge in your life, give yourself an edge by acknowledging your learning disability or your learning style. You can use these tricks to help:

Sit in the front. The fewest distractions are in the front of the classroom, and you are in full view of the teacher. This can help you stay focused and lessen the temptation to be sidetracked. In front, you can see and you can be seen.

Take notes. Of course, having notes to review after class will help you when you go to complete assignments, but just as important, taking notes keeps you focused and will keep you from becoming distracted. If you have trouble taking notes, you can ask the teacher for a copy of the notes, tape the lecture, or have someone else take notes for you. This helps get the information for review, but it doesn't help you stay focused in the room. If you like to doodle, draw images that are related to the material presented. Cartoon figures representing the material presented can keep you on track and can act as reminders of content.

Structure rewards. We all love rewards or prizes and many times those with ADHD don't get them as often as others. Give yourself prizes or rewards. When you are working, schedule one or more breaks. Do something you really enjoy during those breaks, but be sure to set a timer so you don't get carried away. Mix the lively with the boring.

Give yourself a reward when you complete an assignment. It doesn't have to be some expensive gift. Often the idea of doing something you love at the end of a task will provide the motivation to keep you working.

Practice Social Skills

The impulsive behavior that is so much a part of ADHD often creates problems in school and with friends. Practice waiting before you say something. It is hard, but can get better with practice. Count to ten, or twenty, or fifty before you say something to a teacher or a friend. Simply waiting will give you enough time to come up with what may be a more appropriate comment. The old saying, "If you can't say anything good about someone, don't say anything," can be helpful.

Talking in the "I feel" voice also helps you get your message across without attacking others. If you can say, "I feel frustrated when you give the assignments so quickly at the end of class," you are more likely to get your teacher to help than if you say, "Why do you have to be such a jerk and give the homework so fast I can't write it down?"

When you are working with your priority system, you will sometimes have to say "no" to your friends. Though going to the movies might be high on your wish list, if you haven't completed at least the ones on your priority list, you may have to postpone your trip to the movie theater. Practice saying, "I would love to go with you, but I am busy with schoolwork tonight." Learning to postpone this type of activity is essential in reaching academic goals.

Practice listening to your friends. Sometimes friends think we don't care about them when we become distracted while they are talking, or interrupt what they are saying. Be sure to look at your friends while you are talking to them or listening to them.

Look for Support Systems

When you are struggling, it is twice as hard when you struggle alone. Look for help. Join a support group. It can be so helpful to talk to others who are going through the same problems. In many schools, guidance counselors arrange groups for students with ADHD. Colleges often have both social and academic support groups. Some even have advocacy groups that can help you develop the self-advocacy skills necessary to get what you need. If you don't want to join a group, at least talk to a friend. Sometimes teenagers with ADHD are reluctant to tell others about their disability. Usually your friends already suspect you have an attention problem. Talking your problems over with a good friend can help.

Get Academic Support

If you have been diagnosed with ADHD, you may already be getting support at school. Tutors and counselors are there to help you. If you are getting ready for college or are in college, you MUST reach out and ask for help. Colleges that receive federal funds are required to offer accommodations for students with ADHD. Visit the Office for Students with Disabilities. Professionals there can help you choose courses and just as important, they often know which teachers work well with students who have learning problems.

Ask for Accommodations

Students with ADHD can have a variety of symptoms and can benefit from a variety of accommodations. Your school's guidance counselor or the disabilities services director can help you find accommodations that work for you. Some students use sophisticated devices like FM amplifiers to help them concentrate. Others have found simple eye contact from the teacher is enough to help them stay focused. Some students need to get out of their seats and move around. Your accommodations may include permission to leave the classroom for a few minutes to release some of the fidgety symptoms associated with ADHD. Talk to the specialists at your school.

> My teacher and I have agreed that when he makes an important point—one that I should include in my notes—he will look directly at me. The eye contact helps me stay focused.
>
> —A community college student

Exercise

Keeping in shape is good advice for everyone. If you have ADHD, exercising can not only keep you in shape but can expend some of that extra energy. If you enjoy team sports and can follow a coach's directions, group activities can provide not only exercise but also friendships. Sometimes those with ADHD find team sports frustrating. Having to follow directions in their relaxation time doesn't help them relax. Instead, it presents an additional level of stress. If this is you, don't involve yourself in organized sports. Instead, work out with a friend. Jog together. Go to the gym together. Shoot hoops. Go ice skating. Find an activity you enjoy and share it with someone.

Know Yourself

If you are going to advocate for yourself, you must understand your learning disability and the strategies that help you succeed. This is the most important self-help tip of all. You can't help yourself if you don't know what you need. The more you learn about ADHD and your particular symptoms, the more you will be able to explain your needs to your teachers, your coaches, and your friends.

Take Responsibility

Teenagers with ADHD are often frustrated; in their frustration, they blame others for their mistakes. "My teacher didn't explain it." "My mother didn't get me up on time." "My father wouldn't let me take the car." If you are to be successful as a young adult, you must stop blaming others and accept yourself for who you are. Those with ADHD aren't the only people who make mistakes. Everyone makes mistakes. Those who accept their mistakes and look for alternative ways of handling problems are the most successful. You can be more successful by saying, "Yes, I made a mistake. This problem is my fault, but I can do things differently next time." Accept the situation and more importantly, move on.

As a young adult, much of the responsibility of managing your ADHD symptoms should be yours. Learn all you can about your disorder, examine the ways it affects you and your social and academic performance, and begin developing a plan for success. Ask for help when you need it. Teachers are often more than willing to help if you let them know in advance that you need accommodations. Practice saying, "I have ADHD and it helps me to learn when I have the list of course requirements in advance" or "It helps me when I have someone take notes for me" or "It helps me when I can record the lesson and play it back." Whatever it is that will help you to learn, you should share that information with your teacher.

If you are on a Individual Education Plan (IEP) in high school, become involved in its development; see the information on Individual Education Plans (IEP) in chapter 10. When you know how your learning disability affects you, you can be directly involved in a plan to help you succeed.

A Word of Caution: Taking Responsibility for Your Actions

Young people with ADHD often have higher rates of alcohol and drug abuse (though a recent study suggests those treated with medication for ADHD may reduce that risk). Because impulse control and inattention are often problems for those with ADHD, teens may take unnecessary risks while driving. In a recent study, research subjects with ADHD were involved in accidents four times more often than those without ADHD, they received far more traffic citations (often for speeding), they were nearly seven times more likely to be involved in two or more crashes, and over four times more likely to be at fault for the accidents in which they were involved.

Are you someone who can listen to the radio, talk to your friends, make a call on your cell phone, and drive at the same time? Most people can't. Limit your activity while driving your car. Be safe.

Poor planning skills can result in a lack of sexual responsibility, putting you at greater risk for sexually transmitted disease and for unintended pregnancy.

All too often, those with ADHD have other learning problems as well. Problems with executive functions can cause reading difficulties, math problems, and social problems too. Other areas of this book cover related learning disabilities that may be creating difficulties for you. Review the information in those chapters as well.

Some students with ADHD and other learning disabilities have problems with depression. Don't ignore this possibility and don't be afraid to get help. Your guidance counselor, your doctor, your school nurse, and your special education teacher can all recommend counselors if you need one.

The Good News

Areas of strength and weakness vary widely among teenagers with ADHD. Many have areas of strength that they feel more than compensate for deficits in other areas.

Researcher Dr. Bonnie Cramond believes that many of those diagnosed with ADHD are also creative. While inattention and impulsivity can be negative traits, Cramond identifies many in history who have found recognition despite their failures to attend to task. She mentions poet Robert Frost, architect Frank Lloyd Wright, and radio inventor Nikola Tesla as three examples of those who had such rich minds that they could

> I've always been able to do more and think faster and in more directions at once than most people....
> Now that I know why, I don't think I could have been as successful without it (ADHD).
> —Michael Zane, founder of the Kryptonite Bike Lock Corporation

Robert Toth says his school days were very sad. With both attention deficit disorder and dyslexia, he had problems with "everything—reading, writing, math." He repeated fourth grade three times, and he didn't learn to read until he was twelve. He says that even then his visual skills were a source of hope and inspiration.

By the time he was fourteen he was still having trouble with academic subjects, but he was also winning prizes for his artistic achievements. "I found I didn't have an attention disorder when I could focus my attention on what I liked most, and with that came the enthusiasm to hyperfocus." He found that when he was involved on hands-on activities and with the inventions he found in *Popular Mechanics* magazine, his problems with attention diminished.

Today Toth focuses his attention on his artwork. He is a painter, a sculptor, and a jewelry designer. Here he is pictured with one of his paintings and his portrait sculpture of Andrew Jackson. The Royal Scottish Museum, the Smithsonian Institution National Portrait Gallery, The Lincoln Center for the Performing Arts, MGM Studios, and the Franklin Institute have purchased his work. His portrait sculptures are often used as awards, including his sculpture of Benjamin Franklin that is presented as the Ben Franklin Award to screenwriters at the Greater Columbus Film Festival.

To learn more about him and to see some of his work, visit his web site at www.RobertToth.com.

Photo by Lee Toth

complete projects in their heads. While those around them believed they were daydreaming, they were actually working on their projects in their minds.

According to Cramond, many of da Vinci's paintings went unfinished because his interests were so varied and diverse. Creative people may not be so much inattentive as distracted by their own creative thoughts.

Dawn Beckley at the National Resource Center on Gifted and Talented has also examined the performance of what she calls "twice-exceptional" students—those students with high ability and with learning disabilities. These students conceptualize quickly, see patterns and relationships readily, reason abstractly, generalize easily, and enjoy the challenge of solving novel problems on their own. Though the children referred to here have learning disabilities, and they may have problems in school, they also have areas of interest and strength where they can and do excel.

Take a close look at yourself. Not every ADHD teenager is going to be a corporate president, or a famous poet, or a world-renowned architect, but every ADHD teenager has areas of strength. Take an alternative look at your learning disability symptoms. You can look at them as hardships, or you can turn them around and see that they also provide some positives. Impulsive

---

REMEMBER

- Know yourself.
- ADHD can affect your executive function capabilities.
- Use strategies to help.
- Set priorities.
- Get organized.
- Stay focused in the classroom.
- Give yourself rewards.
- Some very talented people in the past had ADHD.
- Some very talented people today have ADHD.
- You have talents too.
- Do the things you are good at and that you enjoy.

people can also be spontaneous people. Those who daydream, dream; your dreams may be a guide to your areas of strength. If you are hyperactive, you probably have more energy than most. Some young people with inattentive symptoms also have hyper-attentive symptoms when they are doing something they are interested in and enjoy. Your ability to focus on those things should be viewed as an asset. Though you need to find strategies to help you overcome those symptoms that make learning difficult for you, you also need to celebrate your gifts and your strengths. Be sure to spend some time each day doing things you are good at. Gifted teenagers with ADHD all too often are over-critical of themselves. Don't let that happen to you. Understand your disability, seek help in areas where help is needed, and recognize and enjoy the things you do well.

Resources

This list introduces a variety of information and opinions about ADHD.

AD/HD Information Center
    http://add.about.com/health/add/cs/allaboutadd/index.htm

ADDvance Magazine
    http://www.addvance.com/

Beal, Eileen J. *Everything You Need to Know about ADD/ADHD.* New York: Rosen Publishing, 1998.

Born to Explore! The Other Side of ADD
    http://www.borntoexplore.org

Children and Adults with Attention-Deficit/Hyperactivity
Disorder (CHADD)
    http://www.chadd.org
    8181 Professional Place, Suite 201
    Landover, MD 20785
    (800) 233-4050
    (301) 306-7070

Hallowell, Edward M., and John J. Ratey. *Driven to Distraction*. New
York: Simon & Schuster, 1995

LDOnline
    http://www.ldonline.org

Nadeau, K. *Help4ADD@High School*. Bethesda, MD: Advantage Press,
1998.

National ADDA
    1788 Second Street, Suite 200
    Highland Park, IL 60035
    (847) 432-ADDA
    http://www.add.org

National Resource Center on Gifted and Talented,
    University of Connecticut
    2131 Hillside Road
    Storrs, CT 06269-3007
    (860) 486-4676
    http://www.ucc.uconn.edu/~wwwgt/nrcgt.html

Dyscalculia:
Problems with Numbers

For students with dyscalculia, homework can be a stressful and overwhelming experience.

Photo by Cheryl Tuttle

How It Feels

Students with disabilities in mathematics are frustrated, they are confused, and they have test anxieties. Their shoulders rise to their ears when they hear the phrase *word problem*. Some have trouble passing math classes. Others have problems with daily living skills. Students told us they had trouble making change or balancing a checkbook. For many, anything associated with numbers makes them feel uncomfortable.

A Definition of Math Disabilities/Dyscalculia

Dyscalculia is a mathematical learning disability in which a person with normal or above average intelligence has unusual difficulty solving arithmetic problems and grasping math concepts. Disabilities in mathematics are not all the same. Some students have trouble with basic calculations, some have problems processing the language of math, some have memory problems that prevent them from remembering or retaining basic math facts, some have visual-spatial problems that cause difficulty, some have problems with small motor control and have trouble writing numbers, and in some cases, those with a math disability may be unable to estimate. About half of the students with disabilities in math also have disabilities in reading, and dyscalculia affects boys and girls in about equal numbers. When a student's ability to perform in math is more than two years behind his or her chronological age, a math disability is probably involved. Disabilities in this area can create minor problems with learning or they can be quite severe.

> I wasn't diagnosed in school and was completely frustrated. When I did math, it frustrated my father to the point where he began yelling .... I didn't have the correct testing to know what was going on. I felt stupid.
>
> —Dana, a third-year college student

You may have a disability in one very specific area of math or you may have problems in many areas. Although much research has been devoted to reading disabilities or dyslexia, research in the area of dyscalculia is not as broad. Researchers have examined this disability since the 1960s, but there is still much confusion about dyscalculia today. Estimates indicate between 6 and 7 percent of the population has a mathematics learning disability. Unfortunately, disabilities in math are persistent. If you had problems with math in fourth grade, it is likely that you still have problems as a young adult today. Since most research has been done on elementary math, little is known regarding disabilities in algebra or geometry.

Dr. David Geary, a psychologist at the University of Missouri and an expert on math learning disabilities, believes that students with learning disabilities in math have problems in three areas:

semantic memory, procedural, and visual-spatial. Those with semantic memory problems have trouble remembering their math facts and often make computational errors. Those with procedural problems use the wrong procedures to solve math problems, and they also have trouble doing the step-by-step tasks necessary to solve a problem. Those with visual-spatial difficulties may rotate numbers, line up numbers incorrectly in a column, or have trouble with the fine motor skills necessary to write the problem. Because geometry is such a visual area of math, those with visual-spatial problems often have particular difficulty with this level of mathematics. Some students are affected by one of these areas. Others may have overlapping problems. As a result, symptoms associated with learning disabilities in math are varied. Most students will recognize more than a few of the following problems:

✳ Problems with basic computation

I believe I have dyscalculia.... For instance, zeros really confuse me. If you were to give me a number such as 082, ask me to remember it, and then later on, ask me to recall what the number was, there's a 99.9% chance I'll tell you one of these ... 802 or 820. In my head, I can visualize the number 082, but when it comes to saying it, I scramble it all up. I now realize it is the reason I depend on notebooks and daily planners for almost everything.... Also, if you give me a problem (even an extremely easy one), I just can't for the life of me picture the numbers in my head ... it has the same effect as talking Chinese to me, and I have no idea what you are saying. But, if it is written down, hurray!

—Vicky,
a college sophomore

✳ Problems with paying attention to problem-solving tasks

✳ Problems with paying attention to instruction

✳ Problems with finding the correct place on worksheets

✳ Trouble with lining up columns

✳ Problems with number confusion (6 and 9, for example, or 17 and 71)

✳ Problems with understanding the basic signs, +, -, %, etc.

✳ Problems with concepts of time and direction

✳ Problems with balancing a checkbook

✳ Problems making change

✳ Problems with music

✳ Poor coordination

✳ Problems with remembering the steps or sequences for sports

✳ Problems with keeping score

✳ Problems with estimating

History of Math Instruction

Early in the 1900s, the focus of mathematics instruction was on basic day-to-day survival skills. Your math instruction might have included making change, taking measurements, reading recipes, and so forth. For most, there was little need for algebra or advanced mathematical skills. By the 1950s, there were significant changes in philosophy regarding math. Imagine how Americans felt when the Soviet Union was the first in space with their satellite, *Sputnik*. In an effort to catch up, federal monies were dedicated to the improvement of math instruction in the United States. Since then, math instruction has bounced between at least two philosophies. One philosophy focuses on the "basics," emphasizing knowledge of basic mathematical operations. The other focuses on a discovery method of instruction, emphasizing relationships and patterns. Unfortunately, students with learning disabilities in math can have problems with either method of instruction.

Causes

Researchers have found that dyscalculia, like most learning disabilities, runs in families. If you have a disability in math, it is likely that your mother or your father has problems in math, too. Depending on the area of difficulty in math and whether you also have problems with reading, areas on the left or the right side of your brain may be affected. If you have a nonverbal learning disability, it is also likely you have serious problems with math.

Some researchers now believe that mathematical problems related to spatial difficulties originate with problems in the right hemisphere of the brain, while problems in the left cause problems with arithmetic operations. According to R. S. Shalev, arithmetic impairment is most profound when there are problems in the left hemisphere. Brain differences may be developmental, meaning this area of your brain was in some way different from birth, or it could be situational, and have come about as a result of an injury.

Some students have problems with math that are related to disabilities in other areas. If you have reading problems, language problems, or handwriting problems, they can contribute to your difficulties in math. The presentation of the math curriculum and the classroom setting can also contribute directly to these problems. Math is taught in a building-block approach. You must fully understand one area before moving to a more advanced area. Unfortunately, in many classrooms, the teacher moves on before all students grasp the basic concepts. Without these foundation skills, you can't make progress. For some, repeated failure leads to math anxieties or phobias that cripple their chances for success.

Coping Strategies

Students with disabilities in math often have memory and organizational problems that contribute directly to their problems with math. As we mentioned above, some have serious anxieties about math. Others have reading issues that contribute to math problems. Some, about half, have no problems in areas outside of mathematics. Finding a strategy for success depends on your areas of strength. Review some of the suggestions below. Because math disabilities differ, specific strategies will be different for each student. Choose the tips that may work best for you.

In the Classroom

Go to class. High school students are required to go to class, but many college students dislike the subject so much they avoid going. You can't understand the information if you don't attend classes.

Take notes. Students often think of note taking for language arts classes, but take few notes in math class. Notes can help you review concepts and procedures and reinforce information presented in class. Start your notes with the title of the lesson. Remember, what instructors say usually has a direct relationship to what will be on a test. If the instructor writes something on the board, it is important. Write it down.

Record the problems. Write down the problems along with each step using the appropriate math symbols. Next to the problem, write the process in your own words. Often, the translation from symbol to your own language will help you understand the problem.

Ask questions. The best time to ask about something you don't understand is during class. Teachers often move ahead when they think everyone has grasped the information. If you don't understand, don't let the teacher think you have. Ask right away. If the teacher is unwilling to take class time for explanations, arrange to meet after school the same day. Don't wait. Often students with math disabilities find concepts easier to understand when they talk about them.

In Your Room

Review your notes as soon as possible. Taking notes helps you store information while you are writing, but more important, if you look at your notes, it reinforces the information. Pay special attention to the titles of the lessons. This may help you see the big picture. If you have time to review your notes during the day, before you get home, that's even better.

Do Your Homework

Do it every day. If you have homework in several subjects, do your math homework first. In high school, homework usually counts toward your grade. If you don't do it, you give away points that you need. Homework problems are usually presented from easiest to most difficult. Start at the beginning and talk to yourself about the specific steps involved in the problems. It may even help to write explanations of the process in your own words next to the problems. If you have good language and listening skills, read problems aloud.

Use graph paper. Do math problems on graph paper or turn standard writing paper on its side to provide columns. This helps keep the correct units in the right place.

Join a study group or get a math buddy. You may want to get the phone number of another student who doesn't mind helping with phone questions when you get stuck. If you still have trouble, make notes of the areas that are difficult and ask questions in class the following day.

Review your entries. If you are using a calculator, review your entries. It is easy to hit a wrong key, and a simple misstep there will result in a wrong answer. It takes a few minutes to do the calculations again, but it is worth it.

Review Your Textbook

Math texts are different. Reading a math textbook is not like reading a novel or even a social studies text. It requires slow review. Preview the section and look quickly at the samples at the end of the chapter. That will help you focus as you then carefully read through the section you have been working on in class. Read the sections aloud. Think about concepts discussed in class or in your notes as you read. Ask yourself questions as you go along. If you have time, it is a good idea to pre-read before the material is covered in class.

Take notes. Highlight new concepts or write them down in your notebook. Look up new terms. Work though the examples provided step by step. Take your time. Again, translate concepts into your own words, or draw pictures or diagrams that help you understand.

Read the textbook hints. Textbooks often provide hints. Review the hints before starting sample problems.

Look at charts and read explanations. These can help you understand the numerical concepts.

Math Center or Resource Room

Visit the resource room or math center. If you are a college student with disabilities in math, the math center on campus should be a regular destination. There are people there to help not only with your specific assignment but also with reducing math anxiety in general.

Keep a list of questions. If you are a high school student, keep a list of questions and sample problems to review with resource room teachers.

Keep a notebook or index cards. Develop a notebook or a set of index cards with formulas or procedures that may help you remember how to do problems in class or at home.

Tests or Exams

Start studying early. Ask the teacher to go over similarities and differences among problems and concepts that will be covered on the test.

Review. If you have gone to class, taken notes, and done your homework, you are in good shape—but you still need to take time to review. Review your notes and see which concepts have been emphasized. Make a list of major concepts. Review homework assignments and quizzes. Look at the similarities and differences among problems in homework. Practice some of each type of problem.

Make a practice test and take it. Most textbooks provide sample tests at the end of each section or chapter. Give yourself the same time limit for your practice test as you will have in class.

Work with a study group or buddy. Try to explain concepts to another student. If you can explain them, you understand them. If you can't, listen as another student explains them to you.

Read instructions. On test day, glance quickly at the entire exam, then look very closely at the instructions.

Do the easiest questions first. That way you can be sure of getting correct answers in the shortest period of time. Among those you feel comfortable with, do those that give the most credit first. That will give you points right away and will leave you additional time for the more difficult problems. If you get partial credit for problems partially solved, at least try to complete them. Clearly write out each step.

Double check your work immediately Do this even if you are using a calculator. If you used scrap paper for your calculations, be sure you copied the information correctly. Ask yourself, does this answer make sense?

Ration your time. If you get stuck, skip ahead and come back at the end if you have time. If you finish ahead of time, take the remaining time to check your work.

Goals

Sometimes, students are encouraged to take lower level math courses in order to survive and graduate from high school. Though the goal of graduation is met, you may not have the necessary background to meet college entrance requirements. If you plan on going to college, your IEP should include accommodations to help you meet those requirements. If you believe basic survival skills are what you will need after high school, your IEP should focus on basic math concepts that will allow you to develop money skills, time management skills, and the ability to measure. Read more about IEPs in the IEP chapter (chapter 10).

Getting Help/ Accommodations

If you need help, ask for:

* Extended time for exams
* A nondistracting environment for exams
* Assignments broken down into smaller components
* Samples of study questions and exam questions
* A scribe to copy problems from the board or from a textbook
* Copies of information written on the blackboard
* Calculators—there are even talking models available (see chapter 15)
* Check Web sites like Study Web: Mathematics Study Skills and Tips (http://www.studyweb.com/links/787.html).

NEVER GIVE UP

We were all put on this earth
To do something:
Teach kids, work in business,
Go to college, the Marines, or the Army.

People may doubt you
And your ability in this world,
But NEVER GIVE UP HOPE,
AND NEVER STOP TRYING.

So prove them wrong
And show them that people with disabilities
Can do anything
Any other person can do!

—Molly Gonzalez, a young adult with dyscalculia

The Good News

Many successful adults had problems with math when they were in school. Some have overcome their math problems by using strategies

Arctic explorer Ann Bancroft had trouble in school. In fact she says her high school years were "miserable academically." Though she graduated and went on to college, her academic problems weren't over. She had difficulty completing her teaching degree, but she knew she "was good with kids" and eventually reached her goal and became a teacher.

Though she no longer teaches in a traditional classroom, she has taken her lessons outside of four walls to inspire students around the world. From November 13, 2000 to February 11, 2001, she and adventurer Liv Arnesen completed a 1,717-mile, 94-day trek across Antarctica to become the first women in history to cross the continent on foot. As they made their journey, they communicated with three million students across the world via the Internet and satellite phone communications.

Bancroft is the first woman in history to cross the ice to the North and South Poles. In 1986 she dogsledded 1,000 miles from the Northwest Territories in Canada to the North Pole and in 1993, she led the four-woman American Women's Expedition to the South Pole, a 67-day, 660-mile ski expedition. Though her learning disability created dark periods in her life, she set goals for herself, achieved her dreams, and continues to be a role model for young people everywhere. You can learn more about her at www.yourexpedition.com.

to help them compensate. Others have sought out careers and activities that don't require mathematics. Polar explorer Ann Bancroft says she was "crummy in math." She says counting on your fingers works "just fine."

Cher has managed to be a successful singer and actor although she can't balance her checkbook. Werner Von Braun became a rocket scientist though he regularly failed his math examinations. Albert Einstein said, "Do not worry about your difficulties in mathematics. I assure you that mine are greater."

Today technology helps many who struggle with math. Calculators, computers, and software programs have been designed to help. Take the advice of Molly Gonzalez, and never give up.

> **REMEMBER**
> - People with math disabilities aren't stupid.
> - Not all math disabilities are the same.
> - Different strategies will help different people.
> - Math skills are like building blocks. Your foundation must be strong.
> - Keep up with your work.
> - Use technology to help you.
> - Check and double check.

Resources

Center for Research in Educational and Adaptive Technology-Assisted Environments

Grand Valley State University

1 Campus Drive

Allendale, MI 49401-9403

(616) 895-6611

dyscalculia@create
   http://www4.gvsu.edu/create/LD/math/dyscalcu.htm

Dyscalculia.org
   8053 N. Delaney Rd.,
   Henderson, MI 48841
   (517) 729-9108
   www.dyscalculia.org

LDOnline
   http://www.ldonline.org

5

Dysgraphia:
Problems with Writing

How It Feels

"Writing is easy; all you do is sit staring at a blank sheet of paper until the drops of blood form on your forehead," said Gene Fowler, a journalist and biographer.

As with most learning disabilities, students who have trouble writing describe feeling dumb, frustrated, and undervalued. They have struggled to form letters, to organize their thoughts and to put them on paper, and/or to spell in a way that other people can recognize. Schoolwork involving writing becomes agony. Many young adults remember staying in at recess time, or staying after school to painstakingly copy work from the classroom blackboard. Most remember having work returned with painful expressions like "sloppy work," "careless," or at best, "good ideas, but messy presentation." By the time they reach high school, essay-type tests and writing assignments are often impossible. The basic paperwork involved with filling out applications can be embarrassing. People don't understand how a young adult can still have trouble just writing an address. Students with these experiences have the writing problems associated with dyslexia or a more specific form of learning disability called dysgraphia.

> I had undiagnosed learning disabilities, dyslexia, dysnumeria, and dysgraphia. All of these difficulties can be addressed. But as a child, I had no idea that I suffered from these problems and no concept even that learning disabilities existed—I believed I was stupid.... Art was my one and only claim to my humanity, to something that made my soul sing.
>
> —Patricia Polacco, award-winning children's book author and illustrator

Definition

In the most basic terms, dysgraphia means difficulty with writing. When a student has no physical impairments, and his or her writing ability falls substantially below expectations, despite average to above average intelligence, the disability may be termed dysgraphia. For some, it means they struggle with letter formation. Others can form the letters, but it takes an excessive amount of time. This struggle to write gets in the way of written expression. As students struggle with the process, they become preoccupied and can't let their ideas and thoughts flow onto the page. Although most people don't even think about the actual process of writing, if you have dysgraphia you understand that the inability to write with ease creates problems with all types of writing. As students get older and the quantity of writing assignments increases, they are often overwhelmed.

> "What do you call someone with bad handwriting?" Answer: A DOCTOR!
>
> I still remember in third grade standing at the blackboard and being used as an example of how not to write. I will never forget the humiliation and subsequent depression that was associated with this.
> —Dr. Fred Epstein, pioneer in pediatric neurosurgery, New York's Beth Israel Hospital (abcNews.com interview)

Causes and Symptoms

As with many learning disabilities, there is a strong indication that it is inherited. Researchers now suspect there is a problem with the interactions between the two main brain systems that allow the translation of thoughts into writing. Some studies indicate that attention problems, memory problems, and fine motor problems are involved. According to the International Dyslexia Association (IDA), "Typically, a person with illegible handwriting has a combination of fine-motor difficulty, inability to re-visualize letters, and inability to remember the motor patterns of letter forms."

The IDA classifies three different types of dysgraphia: dyslexic, motor, and spatial. See the chart. The common factor in all types is poor handwriting, but spelling skills, speed of writing, and drawing skills vary according to type.

The problems created by dysgraphia are difficult, but they are further compounded by the fact that the difficulty in physically forming letters causes the writer to get stuck. When letter production is automatic, memory space is available for the creative process—deciding what to write about and how to write it. Without this "handwriting automaticity," it may be extremely difficult for you to write creatively when you are bogged down in the process.

Although many students learn other skills best with the physical process of writing, if you have a writing disability, writing just makes things more difficult. You may find that even after just copying information, you don't remember the content.

Students who have ADHD (chapter 3) often have problems with written tasks. If you have ADHD, you may find that your thoughts get ahead of your ability to organize and sequence them on paper. And, as would be expected, students with language processing weaknesses often have problems with written language as well.

TYPES OF DYSGRAPHIA AND SYMPTOMS

Dyslexia Dysgraphia
- illegible writing, especially when spontaneous writing is complex
- poor oral spelling, but drawing and copying of text is relatively normal
- finger-tapping speed (a measure of fine-motor skills) is normal

Motor Dysgraphia (motor clumsiness)
- illegible writing
- oral spelling normal
- drawing may be problematic
- finger-tapping normal

Spatial Dysgraphia (problems understanding space)
- illegible writing
- normal oral spelling
- finger-tapping speed normal
- drawing is problematic

Adapted from IDA Fact Sheet #982

Strategies for Success

By the time you are a young adult, strategies geared at improving the quality of your handwriting are "too little, too late." Instead, it is probably best to focus on ways to organize your thoughts, improve your keyboarding skills, and to seek accommodations designed to let your talents shine despite your handwriting problems. Because each student is different, these are just suggestions. They are not a one-size-fits-all solution. Try some. See which ones work best for you.

Visit the Writing Center or Work with Your Special Education Teacher

If you are still in high school, seek the help of your special education teacher as soon as possible. When you first receive the assignment, let your teacher know and plan your strategy together. If you are a college student, go immediately to your school's writing center. There are people there who can help you each step of the way. Purdue University has an excellent Online Writing Lab for college students that can help you organize your thoughts, create a draft, work on your spelling, and more. Check it out at http://www.owl.english.purdue.edu.

Organizing Thoughts

For many students with dysgraphia, writing maps or graphic organizers can help with the organization of information. You can create a template on your computer, or ask your teacher to create one and keep copies in your notebook so you can scan it into your computer. There are many types of organizers (see one sample in figure 5.1). Ask your teacher to show you other organizers that can help you.

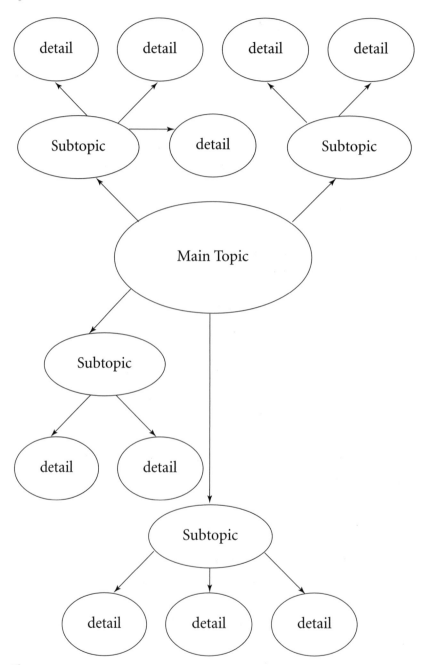

Figure 5.1
Graphic organizers like this one can help organize information before writing.

Keep a List of Words That You Might Misspell

Refer it as you write. Type your draft into your computer. If your teacher will accept and correct drafts, submit your draft for comments. Edit your paper, use your spell checker, and then use a human spell checker. Electronic spell checkers don't catch everything. Always proofread your final project after a delay. When we read immediately after writing, we read what we wanted to write rather than what we actually put on the paper.

P	Plan
O	Organize your thoughts and ideas
W	Write your draft
E	Edit your work
R	Revise your work, producing a final draft

—Regina Richards

Educational therapist Regina Richards uses the acronym POWER to help students organize their written work.

There are many Web sources with excellent tips on organizing, creating rough drafts, and creating term papers. A list is included at the end of this chapter.

Learn Keyboarding Skills

If you don't already have keyboarding skills, take a class *now*. Many students with dysgraphia have problems learning these skills and often come up with creative adaptations of standard touch-typing skills. Once they have mastered their keyboard techniques, the writing process is liberated from the handwriting process. Practice each day, even if it is only for a few minutes.

Assistive Technology

There are so many innovations to help students with writing problems: tape recorders, specialized word processing systems, spell

Patricia Polacco

It's hard to believe that two of the best-known writers for young people had trouble with writing in school. Both Patricia Polacco and Avi have dysgraphia, but they have found ways to cope that have helped them become best-selling authors.

Polacco didn't learn to read until she was 14 and writing was a struggle as well. Fortunately, she had strengths in other areas that helped her cope with her disabilities.

"I had undiagnosed learning disabilities, dyslexia, dysnumeria, and dysgraphia. All of these difficulties can be addressed. But as a child, I had no idea that I suffered from these problems and no concept even that learning disabilities existed—I believed I was stupid. . . . Art was my one and only claim to my humanity, to something that made my soul sing."

Though she studied art in school and worked for an art museum for a time, she did not begin writing and illustrating children's books until she was 41 years old. Today she is an award-winning author and illustrator and has published more than thirty books for young people. You can learn more about her on her web site www.patriciapolacco.com.

Avi

Avi struggled in school as well. In fact, while he was in high school he failed all of his classes. This award-winning writer has dysgraphia. He worked hard. He did his best. Still, he wasn't successful in the classroom. With the help of a tutor, he eventually graduated from high school and went on to college. But he still can't spell. He still makes mistakes when

he is writing his books. Today's technology is of some help. "One of the problems with dysgraphia is pretty bad spelling, so having a spell checker made an enormous difference to me. It also means a neater and cleaner manuscript, and that's nice to have."

But, spell checkers don't catch everything. Sometimes Avi reads his material out loud in hopes of catching mistakes. Sometimes he changes the margins on his typed pages, hoping that a different view of the material will help him spot errors. Avi revises his manuscripts many times before submitting them to the publisher. Editors there can catch any mistakes Avi might have missed.

Knowing how it feels to have dysgraphia, Avi often asks to meet with students with learning disabilities when he goes on school visits. He shares his manuscripts with them, showing them all the corrections on each page—misspelled words, letter reversals, proper nouns or sentence beginnings without capital letters. He wants students to know that although writing problems can be enormously frustrating, his dysgraphia hasn't ruled is life. That Avi has trouble with spelling is a fact, but what is important is that he writes wonderful stories that young people love to read.

Despite his dysgraphia, Avi has published more than forty books for children and young adults. You can learn more about him on his web site, www.avi-writer.com and in Lois Markham's biography *Avi*.

Palacco photo by Klein/Skylight Photography
Avi photo courtesy of HarperCollins

checkers, and so on. Read more about those designed specifically for writing problems in the Assistive Technology chapter (chapter 15).

Accommodations

Students identified with writing disorders or dysgraphia may qualify for accommodations in the classroom. Talk to your special education teacher or the disabilities services coordinator to arrange for accommodations. Listed here are some examples of accommodations that can make your life easier and more fulfilling.

Note taking.

✳ Tape classroom lectures. This frees you from the burdens of writing notes and allows you to review by listening

✳ Take a word processor to class. You can type your notes directly into the word processor.

✳ Request a note taker. A note taker will provide you with a copy of his or her notes.

✳ Ask a teacher for a copy of information presented on the blackboard or on overhead projections.

Spelling. Spelling should not be counted against you on drafts or on written tests. With sufficient time for editing and spell checking, you should be able to produce final projects with appropriate spelling. Use a spell checker, electronic or human.

Test and assessment modifications.

✳ Extra time should be provided for all written work and especially for tests that require writing.

✳ Request oral presentations of assignments rather than written assignments.

✳ Request oral rather than written tests.

✳ Request a reduced amount of written work.

✳ Use a scribe to record answers.

Balance work. Choose your courses carefully. Balance those that you want to take that require writing with those that require little writing. Don't take several writing-intensive classes at once.

Plan time for fun. Often students with learning disabilities have to spend so much time on school work that they don't have time for the things they really enjoy. Plan time each day to do something you love to do. You may use it as a reward when work is completed, or you may just build time into your day for opportunities to have fun. Since struggles cause stress, allow yourself time for some exercise, too. Exercise is a great stress reducer.

The Good News

As with all types of learning disabilities, there are many people who have achieved great success despite their problems. Some think of it as overcoming a disability; others prefer to think of it as using the gifts that often accompany a disability. Award-winning children's book author and illustrator Patricia Polacco believes art gave her an opportunity to excel and encourages others with disabilities to explore their creative talents. Another award-winning author, Avi, struggled with dysgraphia in school and still has writing and spelling problems today. Though he struggled in school, he hasn't let his disability get in the way of his success. He uses today's technology to help him release his creativity and to overcome his problem with spelling.

Although Rhodes scholar Tom Gray struggled with dysgraphia and with failures in school, he received one of the most prestigious academic awards during his senior year at Amherst College. Gray joined an elite group of winners who received scholarships to the University of Oxford in England. As a Rhodes scholar, Gray was recognized for high academic achievement, integrity of character, a spirit of unselfishness, respect for others, potential for leadership, and physical vigor.

Dr. Fred Epstein, a pioneer in pediatric neurosurgery at New York's Beth Israel Hospital, was humiliated as a child because he couldn't write. Today, he is the director of the Institute for Neurology and Neurosurgery and is famous around the world for his pioneering work in brain stem and spinal cord surgery.

Let these people be an inspiration for you. Don't let your struggles and your difficulties get in the way of your dreams and your goals. You may never get an A on a high school term paper, but you can always be creative and talented in other areas. Keep working and keep dreaming.

> I was a poor writer. When I got to high school, I failed all my courses.
>
> One of the problems with dysgraphia is pretty bad spelling, so having a spell checker made an enormous difference to me. It also means a neater and cleaner manuscript, and that's nice to have.
>
> —Avi, award-winning author of books for children and teenagers

Resources

The International Dyslexia Association, International Office
    8600 LaSalle Road, Chester Building, Suite 382
    Baltimore, MD 21286-2044
    Messages (800) ABCD123, Voice (410) 296-0232,
    Fax (410) 321-5069
    http://www.interdys.org

LDOnline
  http://www.ldonline.org

How to Write a Research Paper
and Survive to Hand It In from
Madonna University Library
  http://ww3.munet.edu/
  library/researchpaper.htm

Purdue Online Writing Lab
(OWL)
  www.owl.english.purdue.edu

How to Write and Revise
a Rough Draft from The
University of Texas
  http://www.utexas.edu/
  students/utlc/handouts/
  1234.html

REMEMBER

- Learn keyboarding skills.
- Use all available technology.
- Don't let letter formation difficulties get in the way of creativity.
- Ask for help—visit the writing center or work with your special education teacher.
- Always spell check—use electronic spell checkers and human spell checkers.
- People with writing problems can be successful.

6

Dyslexia:
Problems with Reading

How It Feels

Mad, cheated, cursed, confused, embarrassed, frustrated. These are all words young people use to describe how they feel about having dyslexia. You may have heard teachers call you lazy or have had classmates call you "retard" or other hurtful names. Most students with dyslexia have had experiences they would rather forget. By the time they get to high school or to college, most have learned to cope with the hostile behavior of misinformed adults and mean-spirited classmates, but too often the damage to confidence and self-esteem has taken its toll. It is important at this stage of your life to recognize that we all have strengths and we all have weaknesses. What you do with your strengths and your weaknesses is what will matter as you become a young adult.

> When I was in public school, I was afraid to read aloud.... I wondered why my sister was smarter.
> —Scott, a college freshman
>
> Mad, frustrated, cheated, cursed, nobody gives a . . .
>
> **The Feeling Box**
> **1998 Teen Conference**
> **LDTeens.org**

The first steps to capitalizing on your strengths and compensating for your weaknesses are to understand your disability and to be able to recognize the strategies that may help you succeed. It is important to remember that not all successes come in academic surroundings. Many people with dyslexia have found coping strategies that have helped them succeed in school. Many now take advantage of laws requiring accommodations that help them learn. Still others find that though they were never what we would think of as successful in school, they are able to find enormous success in business, entertainment, and artistic careers that allow them to capitalize on their gifts.

A Definition

The term *dyslexia* comes from the Greek language—"dys" meaning poor and "lexis" meaning word or language. Dyslexia is the term commonly used to describe the language-based learning disability that creates problems in reading, spelling, writing, speaking, and/or listening. Although there is no standardized definition of the term, the World Federation of Neurology defines it as a disorder manifested by difficulty in learning to read despite conventional instruction, adequate intelligence, and sociocultural opportunity. For those with dyslexia, there is a discrepancy between intellectual ability and reading performance.

According to the Learning Disabilities Association (LDA), "reading is getting meaning from print." For those with dyslexia, "getting the meaning" is an ongoing struggle. Difficulties associated with dyslexia fall into several areas.

Phonemic Awareness

Dyslexia often affects understanding and accessing the sound structure of language. This is called phonemic awareness. If you have dyslexia, you may have trouble breaking words down into their separate sounds or segments of speech, called phonemes (pronounced *fo neems*). You may also have difficulty connecting those sounds to written letters. These problems create a barrier between the spoken word and the written word. Without the ability to blend sounds, reading becomes extremely difficult. The more syllables in the word, the more difficult. To make matters worse, those who can't create the sounds can't store the phonological information while reading. Then, because it isn't stored properly, it can't be recalled adequately. See the section on Working Memory below.

By the time you graduate from high school, you should know about 45,000 to 60,000 words made up of the phonemes that create so much trouble.

Rapid Naming

Another area that causes some difficulty for those with dyslexia is the ability to name objects quickly, "rapid naming." If you have dyslexia, your difficulties may stem from an inability to access and retrieve verbal labels for visual information. The connection between a visual symbol and a spoken word must be made in order for reading to take place.

Working Memory

Problems with working memory also contribute to poor reading, comprehension, and note-taking skills. Working memory allows us to put information in the proper sequence and to hold it in there long enough for it to be useful. Problems with working memory can present basic reading problems, making it difficult to string together the correct sequence of letters to make a word.

The same problem can make it difficult to keep words in a sentence in the proper order. This order is called syntax, and without it, it is easy to get confused. The difference between the two newspaper headlines "Man bites dog" and "Dog bites man" is significant. You can see how improper syntax could create major problems.

Your working memory also allows you to understand a sentence by holding the verbal information in your mind long enough to understand the meaning and sequence of the words. Then, you must file it away for long-term storage in order to be able to retrieve it well enough to answer related questions.

In order to get the most out of reading, you must be able to do all the things in the list "Requirements for Reading" on page 105. Reading is complex. Problems with phonemic awareness, rapid naming, and/or working memory can contribute to difficulties in understanding and using language. The complexity of it relates to the different types of problems you may have. You may not be able to decode the words and can't understand for that reason. You may be able to decode the words, but not quickly enough to link them together in a meaningful way. Or you may be able to read and link the words, but have troubling storing and recalling the information.

Although young people with dyslexia often feel they are the only ones struggling with reading problems, they are not alone. Dyslexia is the most common learning disability, affecting between 3 and 6 percent of school children. According to the International Dyslexia Association (IDA), 2.4 million students have been diagnosed with learning disabilities. Of those, between 80 and 85 percent have deficits in language and reading. Their figures indicate that between 15 and 20 percent of the population has a reading disability. You are not alone.

Students with the most significant disabilities are usually identified in elementary school. Others are able to handle the reading associated with the early years but are identified when they have problems with reading comprehension in high school. The sooner problems are identified, the sooner remediation can begin.

REQUIREMENTS FOR READING

- Focus attention on the printed marks and control eye movements across the page
- Recognize and break down the sounds associated with the letters
- Understand words and grammar
- Build ideas and images
- Remember the sequence of the words
- Compare new ideas to what you already know
- Store ideas in memory
- Develop an adequate vocabulary

Recent research indicates that new teaching strategies emphasizing phonemic awareness can help young students as they begin to learn to read. Hope for early identification comes from a recent study predicting dyslexia in newborns. Psychologists Dennis and Victoria Molfese at Southern Illinois University found some infants responded more slowly to taped syllables like "dee" and "bee." The children were tested for dyslexia eight years later. Eighty percent of those diagnosed with dyslexia showed the slow response trait as infants. Researchers hope this type of study will lead to even earlier treatment and will prevent "years of reading failure in school."

Common Symptoms

If you had trouble learning to read in elementary school, it is likely you still have those problems as a teenager. The most common symptoms for high school and college age students are:

* Reading slowly
* Problems with spelling
* Problems with summarizing and outlining
* Poor vocabulary
* Poor comprehension and recall of information
* Problems with taking notes, outlining, summarizing
* Problems with concentrating while reading
* Problems with organizing and completing written projects

Associated difficulties may also include:
* Trouble with identifying the main idea
* Problems with remembering what has been read
* Problems with answering open-ended questions
* Reading words or letters out of sequence
* Skipping words or lines
* Poor memory skills
* Difficulty with abstract concepts
* Problems with time management
* Problems with completing assignments, or completing assignments but not turning them in

The range and severity of symptoms is enormous.

Causes

In many cases, dyslexia is inherited. It is not uncommon for members of the same family to share the disorder. In fact, many adults who have never been diagnosed with dyslexia become aware of their own disability when their children are diagnosed. Some studies have found that as many as 50 percent of children with dyslexia have family members with the reading disability. To date, two specific genes have been associated with the disorder.

NEUROLOGICAL DIFFERENCES

Brain activation patterns now provide us with hard evidence of a disruption in the brain regions responsible for reading—evidence for what has previously been a hidden disability.

—Dr. Sally Shaywitz, codirector of Yale University Center for the Study of Learning and Attention Disorders

Those with dyslexia were once thought to be stupid, lazy, or unmotivated. Now we know none of that is true. In fact, those identified with dyslexia are often identified because they have gaps between their abilities and their performances. Those with dyslexia are as bright as other students; they simply process information in a different way. According to the National Institute of Mental Health, people with dyslexia do not use the same neural networks as normal readers. Scientists now believe dyslexia is neurobiologically based, and new brain imaging techniques now make what was once an invisible disability, visible. Read more about this in chapter 2.

To make matters worse, it appears our native language, English, provides an additional hurdle. Though reduced neural activity during reading is common in all who suffer from dyslexia, it now appears that the regularity of a language's writing system (orthography) also plays a role in the difficulties faced by those who have dyslexia. Because our writing system is so complex and has so many irregularities, it presents a greater challenge to those with dyslexia. Rules that govern the pronunciation differences in words like "pint" and "mint" or "cough" and "bough" make it difficult to figure out the rules governing pronunciation. Researchers who studied the complexity of English, French, and Italian in its relationship to the severity of dyslexia symptoms concluded that English was the most complicated language, Italian the least, and French fell somewhere in between.

Coping Strategies

Studies confirm that brain differences, not laziness or stupidity, are responsible for the reading problems associated with dyslexia. If you have been diagnosed with dyslexia and are not succeeding in school, you may qualify for special services through high school and for accommodations in college. If you are still in high school, you can seek help from teachers who specialize in helping students with learning disabilities. In college, you will need to register with the disability services coordinator at school to arrange for accommodations. Since each student with dyslexia is different and has different strengths and weaknesses, no set formula can be used to help every student. The strategies listed here have helped other students with dyslexia. Select the ones you think will be helpful to you.

Reading a Text

❋ Read the headings in each section.
❋ Look at the pictures and graphs.

✳ Examine the explanations.

✳ Review answer sheets, study guides, and outlines.

✳ Use colored highlighters; use one color for major concepts, another for supporting details.

✳ Look for topic sentences to help you understand what the paragraph is about.

✳ Write a summary of what you have read.

✳ Review the highlighted areas and your summary.

✳ Read what you need. Not all books need to be read from cover to cover. Focus on the information the teacher is emphasizing.

✳ Allow extra time. Reading will take you longer than it takes your friends. You need to accept that as a fact of life and allow yourself more time for homework and reading assignments.

✳ Request books on tape. If reading is just too difficult, request your text on tape. Those diagnosed with serious disabilities in the area of reading usually qualify for books on tape.

Remember, listening to tapes can take much longer than scanning, so again, allow extra time. If possible, take notes as you listen and then review your notes. If you are listening to a novel, try to read along. Books on tape are available on loan from the Recordings for the Blind and Dyslexic (RFB&D) and the National Library Service for the Blind and Physically Handicapped (NLS). For more information, see chapter 15 (Assistive Technology).

Taking Notes and Writing

In class and with homework assignments, taking notes helps you remember information. If you are still in high school, you can ask your special education teacher to help you with note-taking techniques.

If you are a college student, the school's writing center or study skills center can provide help. Here are some strategies that have helped other students:

Use graphic organizers. Some students like to use the divided page method of note taking, recording major concepts on the left and details on the right. Some like to use a web format. (See the strategies section of chapter 5 for an example.) Here, major concepts are in the center of the web and details are placed in areas surrounding the center. Some students take notes with drawings and then use those pictures to help them remember the information. If you use this method, it is essential to translate your picture notes into written notes as soon as possible.

Listen and watch for teacher clues. Most students with learning problems find it helpful to sit in the front of the class. This helps them stay focused and gives them a good view of the teacher's expressions and gestures. Often these gestures and expressions give visual clues regarding what is important. Sometimes they even say, "This is important, so write it down." Believe them and write it down!

Use a tape recorder. Some students need to tape their classes, rather than taking notes. If you use this method, be sure to allow yourself plenty of time to listen to the tapes. Remember, it will take you longer to relisten to a taped lecture than to review notes. Some tape players allow for a higher speed playback (without distortion) that will allow you to move through the tape more quickly. (See the information on technology in chapter 15.)

Use a note taker. Some students with dyslexia qualify for note takers. Another student will take notes and a copy of those notes will be provided for you. Again, the notes only have value if you review them.

Use your word processor. Use a word processor for writing assignments and be sure to use the spell checker. Once you have used your computer's spell checker, use a human spell checker as well. Ask a friend to read your papers for the typos and misspellings all spell checkers miss. See more about note taking and writing in the dysgraphia chapter (chapter 5).

Time Management

Students with developmental reading problems often need more time to compete reading and writing assignments. Your special education teacher can help you work with your academic teachers to arrange a realistic assignment schedule. If you are in college, the disability services coordinator can help. Remember, college students must register with their school's disabilities office in order to receive accommodations. Do it sooner rather than later. It is best to ask for help before you fail that first assignment.

Balance your schedule. If possible don't take more than one or two classes that have large reading components in a semester.

Do your reading assignments first. Try to schedule your homework so that you complete your reading assignments at your most productive time. Don't put it off.

Get a head start. Many teachers in both high school and college provide a reading list or course syllabus before the course begins. Start reading before work is assigned.

Take a study skills class and visit the study skills center. Make yourself a regular visitor at the study skills center at your school. If you are in high school, you probably have time scheduled into a resource room for support. You will need those resources even more at the college level. If you have a paper to write, visit the writing lab when you first get your assignment. Don't wait until the week or the day it is due.

Use a day planner or organizer. Keep track of and prioritize the assignments.

Foreign Language

For many students with dyslexia, foreign language courses are among the most difficult. If this is the case for you, read chapter 7 on foreign languages.

Social Skills

Remember to say "thank-you" to those who help you. It is a simple thing, but teachers, tutors, the staff in the writing lab, or a friend who shares notes will all be more supportive if you remember to let them know you appreciate their help.

Pursue Pleasure

Students with all types of learning disabilities need to spend more time on schoolwork than typical students. Often, they forget to spend time doing things they do well and that they enjoy. If you are good in art, take an art class or make time in your day to draw or paint. If you love music, make time for it in your life. Struggles are always more manageable if we can reward ourselves with activities we enjoy.

Because stress is always an issue for students with learning disabilities, be sure to allow yourself time to exercise. Whether you like a game of pickup basketball or prefer swimming laps in a pool, a physical outlet can reduce stress and leave you better able to face the challenges of reading.

Take Advice from Experienced Students

Try reading Jonathan Mooney's *Learning Outside the Lines* or visit Brown University's Web site and review their students' perspectives on learning disabilities at http://www.brown.edu/Welcome/advice/disabilities.html.

The Good News

Ron Davis, in his book *The Gift of Dyslexia: Why Some of the Smartest People Can't Read and How They Can Learn,* says that those with dyslexia have minds that work in a specialized way. He believes there is a relationship between the minds of dyslexics and the minds of geniuses and that you have been given gifts along with those negatives that are so often the focus of your learning. Although all students with dyslexia are different, with a variety of strengths and weaknesses, Davis believes they share some common mental functions that endow them with intelligence and creative ability. He says those with dyslexia:

1. Can utilize the brain's ability to alter and create perceptions
2. Are highly aware of the environment
3. Are more curious than average
4. Think mainly in pictures instead of words
5. Are highly intuitive and insightful
6. Think and perceive multidimensionally (using all the senses)
7. Experience thought as reality
8. Have vivid imaginations

Magazines, newspapers, television programs, and learning disabilities Web pages are filled with examples of individuals who have excelled either despite, or as Davis believes, with the help of, dyslexia. Charles Schwab, who now runs one of the world's most successful brokerage firms, read Classic comics in order to complete his high school reading assignments. Schwab realized he was dyslexic when one of his children was diagnosed with the disorder. Motivated to help others, he and his wife established the Schwab Foundation for Learning to inform others about dyslexia.

> The real fear that I have for dyslexic people is not that they have to struggle with jumbled input or that they can't spell, but that they will quit on themselves before they get out of school.
>
> —Stephen Cannell, Emmy-winning television writer-producer

Emmy award–winning writer Stephen Cannell, who also realized he had dyslexia when his child was diagnosed, selected his college courses by interviewing professors to find out which emphasized spelling. If spelling was important, he wouldn't take the class. Today, he says, he is "very visual. That means nothing in school, but when I write my books or my scripts, I am seeing everything in my imagination." He acknowledges that reading is hard, but says for dyslexics there are other things they can do well.

Actor James Van Der Beek has dyslexia and he is one of the stars of *Dawson's Creek*. Paul Orfalea, whose nickname was Kinko, had a teacher who described him as "dumb as stone"; in 1970, he started the copy shop that has developed into the lucrative chain, Kinko's.

Academy Award–winning actress Whoopi Goldberg has dyslexia. Erin Brockovich does too, and she offers some excellent advice. Speaking at Penn State's Distinguished Speaker Series, she said, "Most people don't know that I have dyslexia. I don't like to be

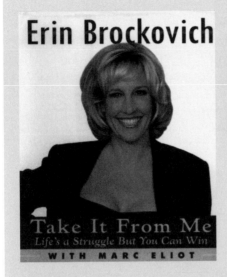

Though Erin Brockovich's legal success was the inspiration for the Academy Award–winning movie starring Julia Roberts, she didn't always feel successful. She, like many other students with learning disabilities, was called stupid when she was in school. When she tried to find work, she wasn't always taken seriously. She had to beg for a job as a file clerk at Masry and Vititoe, but her curiosity and determination uncovered the fact countless people in and around Hinkley, California, had been exposed to toxic Chromium 6 when it leaked into their groundwater from the nearby Pacific Gas and Electric Company's compressor station. Brockovich's work resulted in the largest direct action lawsuit of its kind when the utility company made the largest legal settlement in United States history—$333 million.

At a recent speaking engagement as part of Penn State's Distinguished Speaker Series she had some advice for students. "Most people don't know that I have dyslexia. I don't like to be labeled. We are taught not to judge a book by its cover, but that's exactly what we do. People called me stupid—I knew I could learn, but I just couldn't learn the way that society wanted to teach me. There are not set answers, just be who you are," she said.

Today, the woman who was called "stupid" as a student has received honors and awards across the country for her work. She continues to work for Masry and Vititoe as the Director of Environmental Research. To find out more about her, read her book *Take It from Me! Life's a Struggle but You Can Win.*

Take It from Me by Erin Brockovich, McGraw-Hill, 2002
Reproduced with permission of McGraw-Hill Companies

labeled. We are taught not to judge a book by its cover, but that's exactly what we do. People called me stupid—I knew that I could learn, but I just couldn't learn the way that society wanted to teach me. There are no set answers, just be who you are."

Resources

Davis, Ronald D. *The Gift of Dyslexia: Why Some of the Smartest People Can't Read and How They Can Learn.* New York: Berkley, 1997.

The International Dyslexia Association (IDA),
International Office
    8600 LaSalle Road, Chester Building, Suite 382
    Baltimore, MD 21286-2044
    Messages (800) ABCD123,
    Voice (410) 296-0232,
    Fax (410) 321-5069
    http://www.interdys.org

LDOnline
    http://www.ldonline.org

REMEMBER

- Having dyslexia doesn't mean you are stupid.
- Dyslexia is the most common learning disability.
- English is a difficult language to master.
- Use strategies to compensate for your reading problems.
- Reading will take you longer than it takes your friends. Allow extra time.
- Take notes, get a note taker, or record lectures.
- Highlight important information.
- Use a computer with a spell checker and a human spell checker.
- Sit in the front and listen for clues.
- Do your reading assignments first.
- Reward yourself when you complete difficult tasks.

LDTeens.org
Sponsored by the New York Branch of the International
Dyslexia Association
    http://www.ldteens.org

Mooney, Jonathan, and David Cole. *Learning Outside the Lines: Two Ivy League Students with Learning Disabilities and ADHD Give You the Tools for Academic Success and Educational Revolution.* New York: Fireside, 2000.

Foreign Languages

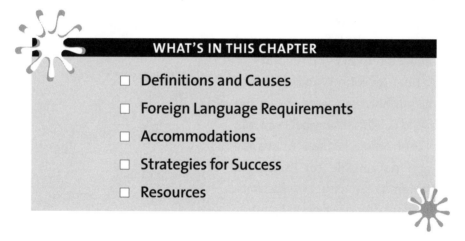

WHAT'S IN THIS CHAPTER

- [ ] **Definitions and Causes**
- [ ] **Foreign Language Requirements**
- [ ] **Accommodations**
- [ ] **Strategies for Success**
- [ ] **Resources**

Definitions and Causes

Although many students have difficulty learning foreign languages, not all students have specific learning disabilities in foreign language. If you have had serious trouble learning a foreign language (despite what you and your teachers consider a sincere effort), if your scores on the Modern Language Aptitude Test (MLAT) indicate you have difficulty in this area, and if you have a learning disability in your native language that affects your reading, writing, or speaking, you may have a foreign language learning disability. If you have a foreign language learning disability, it is likely you also started talking later than usual, had trouble learning to read, and/or struggled with phonics or with grammar and spelling. It also likely that you have someone else in your family who has learning problems in those areas.

As early as the 1960s, foreign language educators suspected students who had trouble learning foreign languages also had trouble with what Paul Pimsleur called "auditory ability" (the ability to distinguish sounds and to decode the symbols associated with those sounds). While many believed lack of motivation, laziness, or anxiety were responsible for failure in foreign languages, Dr. Kenneth Dinklage didn't believe it. He studied high achieving students at Harvard who were having trouble passing foreign language classes. He found the students highly motivated and that, if they had anxiety associated with foreign language, it came *after* failure, not before. He found many of the students had disabilities related to dyslexia. They had trouble learning to read and to spell, they reversed symbols and letters, they confused sounds, and they had trouble with verbal memory. Studies since then have shown a correlation between the level of strength in native languages and grades in foreign language. Those with significant strengths in their native language abilities get the best grades in foreign languages. As with all learning disabilities, the

> *Perfer et obdura; dolor hic tibi proderit olim.*
> Be patient and tough; some day this pain will be useful to you.
> —Ovid

> *L'obstacle nous fait grands [...]*
> Obstacles make us great ...
> —André Chénier

> *Assiduus usus uni rei deditus et ingenium et artem saepe vincit.*
> Constant practice devoted to one subject often outdoes both intelligence and skill.
> —Cicero

severity of the disability can range from mild to quite serious.

Foreign Language Requirements

The ability to speak more than one language is a lifelong asset that has

A disability in foreign language learning is not caused by

- stupidity
- lack of motivation
- anxiety

benefits in both academic and social areas. Learning a foreign language enhances English and other academic skills, and multiyear foreign language study may improve scores on college entrance exams. Some of the most profound benefits of knowing a second language are societal. If you can speak a foreign language, you will have more job opportunities, you will be able to communicate with

Figure 7.1
Learning a foreign language is difficult for many students with learning disabilities. If you have a learning disability in your native language that affects your reading, writing, or speaking, you may have a foreign language learning disability.

Photo by Penny Paquette

more people, you will have the opportunity to fully appreciate travel opportunities, and you will improve your cultural exposure and understanding.

Most students (yes, even those with learning disabilities) can learn a foreign language. For many it is a struggle, but it is a struggle with substantial benefits. In addition to the advantages listed above, high school students with a foreign language background have a greater chance of success in college-level foreign language classes. Many colleges require high school foreign language study for admission. Whether you want to improve your job opportunities, enjoy cultural exposure, or get ready for college, the study of foreign language in high school has major benefits. Still, for many with learning disabilities, foreign languages don't come easily. Don't give up just because it is hard. As an LD student, you know things are often more difficult for you. If you are still in high school, your learning disabilities teacher can help you find strategies to use in your foreign language class. Your foreign language teacher can provide accommodations to help you succeed. Some students are more successful in languages that require more speaking than reading. Others excel in classes that require more reading. Talk to your LD teacher about which might be best for you. Some high schools offer waivers of graduation requirements for those students who have been unable to pass high school courses. Though this might seem like the easiest way out, it has some major disadvantages if you plan on going to college. Some colleges require high school foreign language success for admission. Others have college level foreign language requirements that may be easier to meet if you have taken foreign language in high school.

Some colleges and universities offer waivers or course substitutions for those with documented disabilities in foreign languages. Although colleges may choose to provide these alternatives, it is important to know that they are not required to provide alternatives

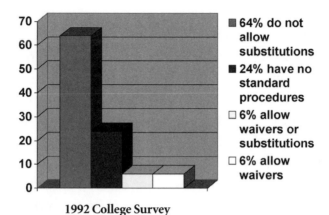

1992 College Survey

Figure 7.2
In a recent survey of college policies, the majority of schools reported that they do not allow foreign language waivers or substitutions.

to foreign language requirements. In a 1992 survey of colleges (Fig. 7.2), 6 percent of the respondents stated they allowed waivers of foreign language requirements, another 6 percent offer a choice between a waiver and a course substitution, 24 percent reported no standard procedures, and the rest provided no substitutions.

These figures indicate the importance of making a thorough college search as well as the importance of speaking to the disability services coordinator at the colleges you are interested in attending. If you believe you will not be able to survive a foreign language course in college, and it is a graduation requirement for the degree you are interested in, you must know if the college will allow waivers or substitutions.

Accommodations

Under Section 504 of the Rehabilitation Act (see chapter 12), colleges are required to provide accommodations to students with disabilities. If you have a documented learning disability, the disability services coordinator can help you receive accommodations in foreign language. This might include a note taker, alternative forms of evaluations (allowing oral or written responses, for example), alternative test formats, extra time for tests, or other modifications of standard procedures. Although not required to do so, some colleges offer alternative foreign language programs specifically for students with learning disabilities. Some also offer tutoring or remediation programs for students with learning disabilities, and as mentioned above, some colleges allow waivers or course substitutions. Many colleges require students to take the MLAT test as verification of a disability. The test is designed to show how easily an individual may learn a foreign language and can provide a measure of foreign language aptitude.

Strategies for Success

One of the best ways to assure success in college is to take a foreign language in high school. Even if it is a struggle for you in high school, you will benefit from the experience in the long run. You may repeat the same levels of the language again in college, but with your high school experience, you will be better prepared for college-level work. If you believe you will struggle, seek out specialized programs designed for students like you.

Both high school and college students should choose a language that best fits their area of strength. If you have strong speaking skills in your native language, look for a conversational foreign language class. Here the emphasis will be more on class participation and discussions than on grammar and spelling. If, however, your speaking skills are weak, you might look for a language that places more emphasis on reading, such as Latin. Some colleges now consider American Sign Language as a foreign language option.

If you decide to apply for a course substitution or a waiver, be ready with documentation of your foreign language disability. Unfortunately, many colleges look for failure in foreign language in high school as a criterion for a foreign language LD. Some colleges require low scores on the MLAT. Requirements for recognition of a foreign language disability vary widely from college to college, but most require extensive paperwork before providing either waivers or course substitutions.

If you struggle with foreign language in high school but would like to take a traditional college-level foreign language class, consider auditing the class for at least a semester before enrolling for credit. If the college allows it, you could also consider taking the class pass/fail. Remember, the more experience you have with the language, the more likely you are to succeed.

The following tips can help you succeed. Because each student is different, not all tips are for all students, but these are basic techniques that should help everyone. Accept that learning a foreign language requires work, but acknowledge that the benefits make it worth the effort. You will make mistakes. Everyone learning a new language makes mistakes. Try to think of mistakes as part of the learning process.

Go to class. Though this seems obvious, many college students

> **REMEMBER**
>
> - The benefits of knowing a foreign language make it worth the struggle.
> - Some colleges require high school foreign language for admission.
> - Colleges may require documentation of a foreign language disability if you need a course substitution or waiver.
> - Not all colleges offer substitutions or waivers.
> - Success requires practice.

avoid classes that give them trouble. If you don't go, you can't succeed.

Go prepared. Allow *at least* a half hour each day (an hour will provide more than double the benefits) for foreign language study. Work everyday. Review the new vocabulary and grammar in your textbook. Write new words on index cards and study them before you begin the written work for the chapter. Write a sentence using each of the new words. Record new verb conjugations on index cards. Practice conjugating them on your computer.

If audiotapes are provided as part of your class, listen to them—not just once but over and over until they begin to make sense. If speaking is a large part of your class, find a partner to practice with. Try to practice dialogs each day. You can do it in person or you can talk on the phone. If videos are provided, watch them. This gives you an opportunity to learn the language by watching and listening.

Visit the foreign language lab. If your school provides help at a foreign language lab, do your homework there. You are sure to find support there and will probably find people willing to practice speaking.

Read a foreign language newspaper or magazine. Ask your foreign language teacher where you can find a newspaper or magazine. Popular, cultural magazines are fun to read and can improve your vocabulary.

Watch foreign language films. Not only is this an entertaining way to spend a few hours, listening to native-language speakers can improve both your vocabulary and your pronunciation.

Resources

Foreign Language Learning Homepage's Tips
http://www.foreignlanguagehome.com/learn.htm

Foreign Language Learning Links to More Tips
http://www.foreignlanguagehome.com/learn8.htm

Foreign Language Resources on the Web
from UC Berkeley Instructional Technology Program
http://www.itp.berkeley.edu/~thorne/HumanResources.html

Tips on Studying a Foreign Language
from the University of Texas
http://www.utexas.edu/utcd/utcd98/services/lsc/handouts/
1705.htm

8

Nonverbal Learning Disability

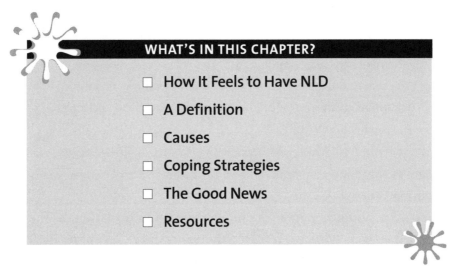

How It Feels to Have NLD

Young people with NLD have been picked on, ostracized, humiliated, left alone, and hurt. You probably have suffered some of the unpleasant consequences of having NLD from teachers or other students. Maybe you were the last one picked every time for teams in gym class, maybe others laughed as they watched you get lost, maybe you couldn't make friends.

Tera Kirk on her Tera's Jump-station Web page talks about some of the difficulties she has had with NLD. Tera mentions problems, but she also recognizes compensations that can be made to achieve success. Like many young people with NLD, Tera has difficulties with facial expressions and describes her "staring spells."

> The biggest struggle for me was always social stuff. It isn't social skills. It was knowing what was appropriate and what was inappropriate. If a friend told me something and didn't say it was in confidence, I didn't know. Making friends was almost impossible.
>
> —Valeska,
> a college student

Actually, for me, these "staring spells" are, I think, a compensation to keep me from being over-whelmed by visual stimuli. . . . It takes me a while to decipher what it is I'm looking at, and if there are too many things to decipher it can cause overload and I need to visually shut down.

Others sometimes misunderstand Tera's staring and believe she is staring at them.

Alice, another young person who posted information on the NLDline Web page, says, "After my experiences in junior high school, I had tried hard to keep everything inside. I have seen psychologists, audiologists, speech-language therapists, and a neurologist. I have learned that I am not a lazy malingerer, stupid, or psychotic." And you are not lazy, stupid, or psychotic either. There are many resources for young people who have NLD. A list of recommended readings and Internet resources is included at the end of this chapter.

A Definition

Nonverbal learning disability (NLD) is a right-hemisphere brain syndrome characterized by deficits in nonverbal reasoning. A diagnosis of NLD includes a discrepancy between verbal IQ and performance IQ as well as academic, social, and emotional weaknesses. Those with this disability have problems getting information from watching and prefer to get their information in written form or verbally. Because more than 65 percent of communication takes place through nonverbal means (facial expressions, gestures, body language, speaking distance, and so forth), those with NLD miss the information that does not come directly through speaking and listening.

At this time, there is no formal NLD classification within the federal special education laws recognizing it as a handicapping condition. In some school systems, students with NLD are identified and served within the "other health impaired" classification. Professionals involved in the study and identification of NLD know that this lack of formal classification leads to misdiagnosis and underdiagnosis and they continue to work toward a specific, educationally acceptable identification system. In the meantime, there is agreement that those with NLD often have problems in the following areas:

Motor Skills

Problems with coordination, balance, and writing are typical. For many with NLD, sports are extremely difficult. The coordination, balance, and muscle movements required for athletic activities just aren't there. Sports-related activities require gross motor skills, those that involve the large muscles in the body. Some of the problems in this area are related to visual-spatial processing discussed later.

Smaller muscles are also involved. Many of those with NLD had trouble learning to tie their shoes. Playing with Legos or other toys with small parts just wasn't fun. Problems with writing are often a problem for young children and may continue into adulthood. Those with NLD have problems taking notes. The graphomotor skills necessary for note taking are affected. If you have NLD, your fingers probably just won't move as fast as your mind. This can become a significant problem in high school and in college.

Visual-Spatial Organization

Visual processing helps us understand how objects relate to each other in space. Those with poor visual-spatial skills have trouble learning from images and can't use visualization as a learning tool.

Maps, charts, diagrams, and similar graphic representations may be confusing or even unintelligible. Although they may provide important supplemental information for those without NLD, they are a source of frustration for those with visual-spatial deficits. Think back. While those around you were thrilled and excited about doing dioramas in elementary school, did you cringe at the thought of that type of assignment? Were you willing to write lengthy papers rather than try to create images in a shoebox?

Visual-spatial difficulties can also make playing sports difficult. In order to catch a ball, you must know where the thrower is, how quickly the ball is moving, how fast you must move to get to the place the ball will land, and so forth. The integration of that type of information can be impossible. If you have NLD, you probably are not an athlete.

Arts and craft activities can also be difficult. Because much of the instruction in these areas is presented visually and students learn by watching what the teacher does, artsy activities can be difficult. Even if you can understand the process, poor motor skills may get in the way of success.

Getting lost is also a common problem. If you have visual-spatial problems, you may have trouble finding your way around. You may need to write down specific directions that help you find your way. Even then, you can become confused. As a result, you may not be eager to visit new places.

The organization needed to perform some math functions is also affected. Lining up columns, recognizing symbols, moving directionally to perform a function from right to left, or the other way around, can be very difficult.

Because you can't actually see time and you certainly can't capture it with words, it can create problems, too. You may find that you miss appointments, or you may be late. This may be because you got lost, but it may also be an inability to conceptualize time.

Getting organized can be a problem, including putting information in order and understanding cause and effect.

Social Skills

One of the most difficult areas for those with NLD is interpreting what people mean, rather than relying solely on what they say. While most people get much of their information from facial expression, gestures, or other nonverbal clues, those with NLD have trouble decoding those visual images. Changes in tone of voice and the rhythm of speech can also be misunderstood. You may have heard someone shout, "Oh, you know what I meant" or "Look at me. Do I look like I am laughing? This isn't funny." Unfortunately, you probably didn't know what the person meant. These subtleties of communication can create problems not only in academic achievement but in making friends as well.

If you can't tell immediately by facial expression if a person is happy or sad or disappointed or angry, it is difficult to know how to approach that person.

Those with NLD like to be given very specific, step-by-step, verbal information. Sarcasm, symbolic language, plays on words, and jokes may be beyond understanding. This makes social interaction difficult.

Because you don't learn by watching the way others behave, you may find yourself making social blunders. If everyone in a group hugs when they meet and you instead shake hands, it sets you apart from the group. You, of course, didn't notice the others hugged as their greeting.

Visual-spatial problems can also affect social relationships. Because it is difficult to recognize your own body's position in space, those with NLD are sometimes accused of "getting in the face" of other people. You may unknowingly stand too close to others, or in an effort to feel secure in space, reach out to touch someone. Not knowing why you are touching them, those around you may withdraw from or misinterpret your touch.

Other Symptoms

Many of those with NLD had great success as young students. If you have NLD, you probably learned to read quite easily, you are probably a master speller, you can memorize with little difficulty. These are all assets that help young children succeed in school. These skills remain valuable as children grow into teens, but the difficulties mentioned above can get in the way of success as you get older.

Because you process information by talking rather than watching, you talk a lot. You may like to talk your way through problems. It may actually make you feel less nervous, so you may talk more when you are anxious. You get your information not by watching, but by asking questions. This is the most logical way for you to find out what you want to know. Others, however, may think you ask too many questions, or that you should understand instinctively, without asking. Because you may be insensitive to the rhythms or tones in speech, your voice can seem flat or without emotion to others. Peers may think you are unenthusiastic or sometimes even boring as a result.

Many of the problems associated with NLD are sometimes classified as impairments in executive functions. Problems may include the inability to make plans, to set goals, to organize and carry out the plans necessary to reach goals, to solve problems, to follow rules, to remember and to learn from past experiences, to learn and obey social conventions, and to place incidents in time and place. Clinical psychologist Dr. Michael Roman believes the incidence and severity of these "executive function" problems are probably more common in severe cases of NLD and "quite rare" in more subtle cases.

Causes

Although Helmer Mykleburst first characterized NLD as a specific type of learning disability in the mid-1970s, the cause or causes of NLD are still under investigation. Deficits in the right side or hemisphere of the brain may be involved. Brain scans of those with NLD often show differences in the right hemisphere. This right side is the area of the brain that can work with both visual and verbal information at the same time. As a result, it can help us read a person's facial expressions and gestures and combine that information with what a person is saying to get a clear understanding of not only what the person says but also what the person means as well. This is the kind of skill that gives those with NLD so much trouble. You can read more about brain research related to NLD in chapter 2.

Sometimes, the differences in the brain have been caused by specific damage as a result of injury, hydrocephalus tumors, radiation, and/or seizures. Still, there is no indication that everyone affected by NLD has suffered a brain injury.

The incidence of NLD is difficult to determine because the disability may often go undiagnosed or misdiagnosed. According to

NLD specialist Sue Miller, between .1 and 1 percent of the general population has the disorder—that's between 1 in 100 and 1 in 1000, a huge range.

Similarities with other disorders may contribute to the problems of diagnosing NLD. According to Dr. Roman, "nonverbal learning disabilities represent a discrete and separate diagnostic entity. However, some of the symptoms identified are similar to those described for other disorders."

Because they share some identifying features, some researchers believe that Asperger's syndrome and autism are similar disorders. Definitions of Asperger's syndrome and autism are included in the glossary section.

As diagnostic research continues, we will learn more about NLD and the number of people affected by it. For you, it will be important that you seek out people who recognize the disorder and who have experience teaching young people affected by it. If your symptoms are minor, you may do just fine on your own; if your symptoms are more significant, you will need help.

Coping Strategies

There is a broad range of symptoms in those with NLD. Depending on how NLD affects your life and your learning, you may find some of these coping strategies helpful. Included here are strategies for those who are still in high school as well as those who are enrolled in college. Social strategies are helpful whether you are in school or in the work force.

Academic/Organizational

Learn to explain your disability. Students who understand NLD are in a better position to ask for accommodations or help than those

SAMPLE ACCOMMODATIONS FOR HIGH SCHOOL

Student will have a second set of books to keep at home.

Student will sit in the front of the class.

Teacher will break down assignments into manageable segments and present them one at a time.

Teachers will allow extra time for tests and tests will be provided in a distraction-free environment.

Student will meet as needed (at least weekly) with counselor to discuss any social problems.

SAMPLE ACCOMMODATIONS FOR COLLEGE STUDENTS

Student may use a calculator.

Student may record lectures.

Teacher will provide copies of any work to be copied from the board.

Student may take tests in a distraction-free environment.

Charts and graphs provided by teacher will include a written explanation of the material presented.

The laws governing accommodations at the high school and college level are different. See chapter 12 (The Law and Your Rights) for more information.

who cannot tell others what they need. Read the results of your tests; review your IEP. If you are still in high school, ask your special education teacher or your psychologist to help you understand your disability well enough to explain it to others. Be sure your IEP provides services in the areas that need remediation—reading comprehension, handwriting, and/or social skills, for example. See the list of sample accommodations in the box above.

Sit in the front of the class. The least number of distractions is in the front of the class. You also give the instructor the impression you want to work hard and are paying attention.

Ask for explanations. Always ask for a verbal explanation of new material. If material is presented in chart or diagram form, be sure it also includes a written explanation of the information. When doing work for school, read the captions below charts and graphs. They usually present the same information in a written format. If you are in a math class, ask for written or verbal explanations of mathematical processes.

Examine handouts. Look at the instructor's handouts. Teachers often give an excellent overview of the material they will present in their handouts. This material usually includes an overview of what you will need to know for tests or assignments. When reading information for the course, pay particular attention to the information the instructor has told you will be important.

Record lecture material. If note taking is too difficult, record lecture material. Because your verbal skills are strong, you can review by replaying the lecture tape. If work is to be copied from the board, ask for a printed copy of the material.

Ask for notes. Request class notes or outlines before lectures, then highlight the important areas, rather than taking notes.

Divide jobs into small parts. Whether reading or writing, break down schoolwork into small segments and take breaks in between.

Ask for oral exams or untimed tests.

Join a study group. Find one that enjoys talking through problems. Remember not to dominate, but participate.

Explore waivers for impossible courses. Although most students with NLD can master basic mathematical calculations and algebra, the visual quality of geometry makes it extremely difficult. In some schools, students can take algebra I and II and skip geometry. Ask if this is an option at your school.

Use a calculator.

Use an organizer. Create a daily schedule and check items off as you complete them.

Use a pencil or an erasable pen. Use a pencil or an erasable pen for note taking and for homework assignments.

Use color to help. Cover your books in recognizable colors—blue for social studies, red for math, and so on. This will help you find the book you are looking for quickly and easily. This also protects your books—an excellent thing for schools and an excellent thing for you if you are in college. It is much easier to sell a college textbook if it is in good condition.

Use color-coded folders to organize your work. You can match colors to texts, so all social studies work is blue and all math is red. All the work for each subject is organized and identifiable.

Read for understanding. When working from a textbook, read the questions at the end of the chapter or the instructor's study guide before you begin reading. Pre-read all the headings, then read the text. As you finish each section, tell yourself what you have just read.

Talk through your assignments. Your strength is in your verbal skills, so use them to help organize your work plan.

Computer use. Use a computer for all written assignments and tests, if possible.

Wear a digital watch. If you still have trouble with a traditional watch or clock, get a digital model and wear it.

Get an extra set of books. Many high schools will provide an extra set of textbooks for students to keep at home. This helps many students with organizational problems.

Learn to outline. Ask for specific help with outlining. Your verbal skills are strong, but your writing sometimes needs direction. Often a special education teacher at the high school level or instructors at a college-level writing center can help you organize your thoughts. Submit first drafts of your papers and ask for specific directions for improvements.

> We did find a graduate student to act as my "human guide dog." She was an intern at a place that taught social skills. She came to campus every week and showed me new routes to places. ... My "human guide dog" was very helpful, but I wish I'd made it clear that she probably shouldn't talk to me about anything other than where we're going. ... I'm thinking really hard here, and don't have the mental energy for stuff like how my day was.
>
> —Tera Kirk

Organize books. Keep the books you need for morning classes in one part of your locker, those you need for afternoon classes in another. Always keep your school and library books in the same place at home.

Finding Your Way

Ask for directions. When going to new places, ask for specific landmarks along the way. Write them down and follow the list of landmarks as you travel to your destination.

Travel with a friend. All of us have friends who have strengths where we have weaknesses. Rely on your friends when you are traveling. They will probably be better at finding new places than you are. Ask for a mentor to help you learn your way around campus. Be sure to explain that you need to concentrate while learning your way around.

Take a practice trip. If you need to go to a new place for a meeting, and going with a friend is not an option, take a practice trip. If time allows, a pre-visit can take the anxiety away from going to a new place on meeting day. You will learn the route and will know how long it takes to get there.

Take a tour of the campus. Take the tour more than once. Campus tours are usually scheduled several times each day. If you take the tour several times, making notes on a simple map, you may find it easier to learn your way around.

Driving. Strengths and weaknesses vary. Many with NLD are just not able to drive. If you can drive, carry directions with you. Type the directions into your computer and print them out in a large type-face. Tape the directions to your dashboard where you can see them easily. If you don't have a computer, write the directions in large block letters.

Making Friends

Join a volunteer group. Often those with NLD have trouble making friends. Volunteer activities present good environments for new friendships. You will share common interests with others there and you will get the benefit of helping those who are less fortunate than you.

Practice listening and asking questions. Sometimes those with NLD talk too much, or at least those around them think they do. Practice listening. That doesn't mean you should sit silently while those around you talk. It simply means you should stop, take a deep breath, and think about what you want to add to the conversation.

Ask questions. Most people love to talk about themselves or add information to a discussion. When you ask a question, you are part of the conversation, but you allow others to contribute as well.

Enroll in social skills classes. If you are still in high school, be sure your IEP includes social skills instruction. Even though nonverbal information does not come to you instinctively, you can learn to improve your understanding and recognition of nonverbal information.

Fashion statements. Though most of us hate to admit it, many people judge others by the clothes they wear. While this may not be an admirable characteristic, it is a fact of life. Because NLDers are often oblivious to the fashion scene, they often wear clothes that set them apart from others, or wear a favorite item of clothing until it is in shreds. Though we all take comfort in a comfortable pair of shoes or a comfortable pair of jeans, taking more interest in your clothes will help you blend in with your peers. Make some time to look at fashion magazines and try to buy one or two items each year that fit the trends. If you have a friend who loves to shop, go shopping together and take his or her advice.

Focus your attention. Those with NLD often have trouble focusing on faces. When you are talking to someone or listening to someone, try to make eye contact. Those without NLD find it disconcerting when the person they are talking to appears to be looking at other things or other people. Always wait until people are finished speaking before walking away (even if you think you know what they are going to say).

Life Skills

Practice being self-sufficient. Practice doing your own laundry, cooking your own meals, and handling your own money. Cooking from recipes can be a problem for many with NLD. If you decide to use a cookbook, keep a pencil handy. Check off each step of the recipe as you complete it. That will help you keep track of what you have and haven't done. If you want to use the recipe again, remember to erase your marks when you are finished with the recipe. A "cooking for two" cookbook can be most helpful. It will provide recipes for smaller portions than most cookbooks. If you are with a friend, you will have enough food for two. If you are on your own, you will have meals for two nights.

Math and money management can be a lifelong problem. If you have a checkbook, choose a design that provides a separate column for each monetary unit. Use a calculator to balance your checkbook. Many computerized checkbook systems do the balancing for you if you enter the proper information. Ask about these at the computer software store.

Work on your visual/social skills. Seek out a therapist or counselor to help strengthen your visual/social skills. Specialists can help you understand the subtleties of body language and help you learn to interpret facial expressions. They can help you fine-tune your facial expressions as well.

Most young people with NLD love to read. Read descriptive passages closely and pay close attention when the author describes a character's expression. For example, "Ron grimaced when he watched Chrissy remove the splinter from her finger" or "Sally smirked when her adversary made a mistake." Think about what a grimace looks like. What does a smirk look like? These facial descriptions can help you recognize them when you see them.

Allow yourself plenty of time. Time is often an issue and those with NLD often find themselves running late. Set an alarm to remind you when it is time to leave and allow yourself extra time in case you get lost. If you don't know how to set your alarm, ask someone to tell you how to do it.

Ask someone. In many cases, "ask someone" is good advice. No one is good at everything and we all need help. Those with learning disabilities often think they are the only ones who need help and are reluctant to ask. If mechanical things drive you crazy, ask someone to tell you how they work. If you don't need to use a tool or piece of equipment more than once or twice, ask someone to do it for you.

Make lists. Make a list of things you need to do and refer to it often. This is helpful for getting schoolwork accomplished, but it is also helpful in the social area as well. Sometimes those with NLD need reminders to help them remember to do the basics—take a shower, brush your teeth, or comb your hair. Do those things first thing each day and do them again before social events.

Use pillboxes. If you are taking medications, you can organize them by day and week in pillboxes available in all drug stores. You can tell if you have taken your pills by simply looking in the individual daily segment of the box.

Don't be quite so trusting. We all like to believe that everyone cares about us and would never do anything to hurt us. Unfortunately, there are mean and dishonest people out there. Because those with NLD take everything so literally, they can sometimes misread sarcasm, teasing, or dishonest behavior. Be cautious.

If you can't say something good about someone, keep quiet. Young people with NLD sometimes say things they shouldn't say. Comments about a person's race, religion, or sexual orientation are inappropriate. Negative comments about another person's appearance are also inappropriate. Stop and think before you say anything.

Stress Management

Seek help. Don't hesitate to call on those who have helped you in the past. Parents often have the best understanding of how you learn and know through experience how to help you.

If you feel depressed or have suicidal thoughts, tell someone immediately and seek professional help. Your guidance counselor at school can refer you to a specialist.

Some students benefit from working with a professional counselor or therapist. Be sure the specialist is knowledgeable about nonverbal learning problems and that instruction includes practical instruction, rather than therapies that rely on insight.

Join a support group. There are others with NLD and they can help you. Guess what? You can help them too. Each individual with NLD is different and has a different set of strengths and weaknesses. Ask the guidance personnel at your school if there are NLD support groups in your area. If so, find out when they meet and get yourself there. You might also check out NLD support groups on the Internet. See the end of the chapter for more information.

Exercise. Swimming is an excellent form of exercise and a pool is an enclosed environment where you can't get lost. With a good sense of where you are going, walking and running are also excellent forms of exercise and can help strengthen coordination. If you are afraid of getting lost, walk or run on your school track, or walk in one direction and then turn around and walk back.

Yoga can help you get in touch with your body. Young people with NLD often look at their bodies as enemies. Yoga can help you tone and concentrate. Deborah Green, author of *Growing Up with NLD*, found Dalcroze training very helpful. It combines rhythm and voice. If you enjoy music, this type of exercise may be fun.

Ride a bike. Again, take a known route or use a stationary exercise bike.

Get plenty of sleep. This is probably one of the most difficult recommendations for high school and college students. Try to go to bed and to get up at the same time each day. Obviously, there will be times when this is just impossible, but acknowledge that sleep makes us less vulnerable to stress and try to stick to a schedule.

Schedule fun. Build activities that you enjoy into your schedule. If you like to watch comedies on television, allow yourself a half hour to watch a program you enjoy. If you can include an activity that helps make friends, even better. If you like to sing, join a chorus. If you enjoy the theater, join a theater group. If you play a musical instrument, join the orchestra or the band. Whatever it is you enjoy, make time for it. Put it on your calendar and do it.

Slow and steady wins the race. If you are a college student, consider a reduced course load. If taking five courses creates such stress in your life that it is impossible to succeed, it might be better to reduce your course load and complete your degree over five years. Of course, this has financial implications, but if your goal is to graduate, it may be worth the additional money to accomplish your goal.

> I always made it a point to go to social events, whether it turned out good or not. At least I made the effort.
>
> —Katie, a college student

> High standards are a wonderful thing to have, but perfectionism is destructive. It's important to have balance in life. It's important to be silly as well as serious, to play as well as work. Without the pressure of perfectionism, real excellence can rise to the surface, allowing success, self-confidence, and happiness to flourish.
>
> —Deborah Green
> *Growing Up with NLD*

Punch out perfectionism. No one is perfect, yet those with NLD seem to try harder than others to be perfect. Ease up on yourself a little. Instead of looking for perfection, look for improvement. Set realistic goals for yourself and take pride in your work when you improve.

Forget failures. Everyone fails at something at some time in his or her life. Accept that everyone fails and when it happens to you, move on. Instead of focusing on the things you have trouble with, look at the things you do well.

Recognize ignorance. Those with NLD have been hurt so many times that they tend to look at themselves as somehow deserving of criticism. Sometimes they forget they deserve the same love and respect as everyone else. What you need to recognize and remember is that most people have never heard of NLD. They don't understand the disability and won't understand your behavior until they learn more about it. That's another good reason for understanding it yourself and for being able to explain it to others. The disabilities specialist at your school can help you inform others about your disability and about your need for accommodations.

The Good News

If you are reading this chapter, chances are that your nonverbal learning disability has been recognized. Many with NLD go undiagnosed or, because they are successful in the early years of school, do not qualify for special education services. Research continues in this field, and every year there is more information available to help those diagnosed with NLD.

In the meantime, take pride in your strong memorization and spelling skills. Recognize that you probably read better than most of your classmates. Remember, you are not alone. To get support from others also diagnosed with NLD, visit the Web sites and read the resources listed at the end of the chapter.

Deborah Green knows what it is like to grow up with NLD. She understands the pain and isolation often associated with the disorder. While in middle school, she had trouble in math, she found it difficult to make friends, she felt clumsy, and she didn't do well in sports. Her problems seemed to get better in high school, but returned while she was in college.

She says she spent a lot of time denying her problems. "Pretending you don't have a learning disability when you're dealing with it every day can be incredibly stressful." According to Green her coping improved when she decided to attack her learning disability head on. She worked on social skills, on her visual/spatial perception, on her coordination through movement. Green is now a teacher.

She enjoys singing and playing the flute and the piano. She loves to garden, and she enjoys reading. She has also become a well-known spokesperson in the field of NLD. She lectures across the country and is currently working on a video about NLD. She is also the author of *Growing Up with NLD*.

To learn more about her, read her book or read her *First Person* comments on LDOnline, http://www.ldonline.org/first_person/first_person.html.

Photo by Ginny Latts

Resources

Green, Deborah. *Growing Up with NLD*. Albuquerque, N.M.: Silicon Heights Computers, 2000.

LDOnline
   http://www.ldonline.org

NLD on the Web
   http://www.nldontheweb.org

Nonverbal Learning Disorders Association (NLDA)
   P.O. Box 220
   Canton, CT 06019-0220
   (860) 693-3738
   http://www.nlda.org

NLDLine
   http://www.nldline.com

Rourke, Byron P. *Nonverbal Learning Disabilities: The Syndrome and the Model*. New York: Guilford Press, 1989.

Tera's Jumpstation
   http://www.geocities.com/
   HotSprings/Spa/7262/

Thompson, Sue. *The Source for Nonverbal Learning Disorders*. East Moline, Ill.: LinguiSystems, 1997

People with NLD can have superb rote verbal memory skills. This means we are able to remember things like song lyrics, word spellings, and new words.... My memory helps me memorize speeches, dates, and definitions.

—**Tera Kirk**
creator of the Web site,
Tera's NLD Jumpstation: A
Resource on Nonverbal
Learning Disabilities by an
NLD Person

REMEMBER

- No one is perfect.
- Not many people know about NLD.
- You may need help with social skills.
- Ask for accommodations.
- Use your strong verbal skills to your advantage.
- Don't be embarrassed to ask for directions.
- Join a group.

Your Test Report

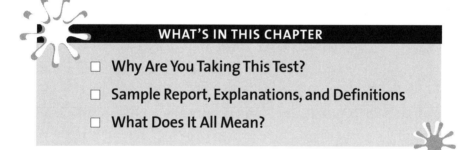

WHAT'S IN THIS CHAPTER

☐ Why Are You Taking This Test?

☐ Sample Report, Explanations, and Definitions

☐ What Does It All Mean?

Why Are You Taking This Test?

Before you can receive special education services in school, you must be evaluated. It's the *law*; you can't get out of it.

If you are receiving services now, you were probably tested in elementary or middle school and possibly retested at a later time. Many students enjoy the tests, but some hate the whole process. Trying to fool the evaluator doesn't work because the people who do the testing have tested hundreds of students just like you and they know all the tricks.

Testing is important because it gives your parents and teachers valuable information about you that they will use to design the best educational program for you. Now that you are older, you should know the results of the evaluations, too.

One reason some students don't like the process is because they are worried about someone "getting inside their heads." Once you understand what the examiner is looking for, you can be an informed participant in the process, and you will feel better about what they might find.

Testing can also be used as a "yardstick." Remember when you were growing taller and your parents used to have you stand against a wall while they marked your height with a ruler? That gave them an indication of your growth over time and compared your growth with that of your brothers and sisters. Testing does the same thing. It lets you know how your skills are growing and how they compare with the growth of the other students in your class.

A test battery should include an individual intelligence test and a test in all areas where you are having difficulty. This might include achievement testing, language testing, motor testing, and tests of your emotions. These tests are given in one-on-one situations to make sure the examiner gets the best possible results. If you take the tests in a group, the examiner doesn't always know whether you understand the directions or even if you are paying attention.

Sample Report, Explanations, and Definitions

This is a sample of a test report. This report is not for an actual student but it is similar to reports of actual students. The major difference is that, for the purposes of this chapter, this student was given many more tests than you would have to take at one sitting and probably many more tests than you would take during the entire evaluation process. The sidebars will explain the different parts of the test.

ANYWHERE PUBLIC SCHOOL
17 Main Street, Dullsville, Your State

Psychological/Speech-Language/Educational Evaluation

Name: Stanley Student
Address: Dullsville, Your State
Date of Birth: 1/3/85
Date of Evaluation: 1/5/01
Age: 16 yrs
Grade: 10th
School: Dullsville
                 High
                 School
Examiner: Dr. Cameron McGrath

> This is information about you. Make sure it is correct. Was Dr. McGrath the one who tested you?

REASON FOR REFERRAL:

Stanley has been receiving special education support since his evaluation in 7th grade. At that time, he had a diagnosis of Executive Function Disorder and Attention Deficit Hyperactivity Disorder. He is currently taking Ritalin for the ADHD and is receiving special education services to help him with written language in academic areas. He is being retested as part of his three-year reevaluation and to determine if he still needs special education services.

TESTS ADMINISTERED

Wechsler Intelligence Scale
for Children—3rd ed.
(WISC-III)
Wechsler Adult Intelligence
Scale—3rd ed. (WAIS -
III)
Stanford-Binet Intelligence
Test—4th ed. (SB-FE)
Woodcock-Johnson Revised
(Cognitive) (WJ-R C)

These measure your basic
intelligence and tell about
your ability to reason.
They measure traits that
have been shown to pre-
dict academic success. IQ
does not usually change,
but it can change in the
case of a student with a
significant learning dis-
ability if the scores are
unduly compromised by
the disability.

Thematic Apperception Test
Incomplete Sentences Test

These tests look at your
emotional state and
adjustment. The results on
these tests are qualitative
(not necessarily number
scores). They are com-
ments about a student's
responses to the test
items and report how he
approached the task. They
are not measured against
or compared to the performance of other students.

There are many other
tests than these. Usually
evaluators have a
favorite test that they
like because they feel it
gives them the best
information. It would
not be possible to list
them all.

Behavior Assessment System
    for Children (BASC)
Achenbach Youth Self Report

These are self-report forms you fill out describing your thoughts, feelings, and actions.

Peabody Picture Vocabulary
    Test (PPVT-III)
Clinical Evaluation of
    Language Fundamentals
    (CELF-3)
Test of Awareness of Language
    Segments (TALS)
Test of Auditory Analysis Skills (TAAS)
Lindamood Auditory Conceptualization Test
Beery Picture Vocabulary Test

These are language evaluations that measure how you understand language and how you express it.

Peabody Individual
    Achievement Test (PIAT)
Wechsler Individual
    Achievement Test (WIAT)
Key Math
Kaufman Test of Educational
    Achievement (KTEA)
Woodcock Reading Mastery
    Test (WRMT)
Woodcock-Johnson Revised
    (Achievement) (WJ-R A)
Detroit Test of Learning Aptitude (DTLA-3)

These are tests of what you know in your school subjects. These scores are quantitative (numbers). They provide objective information that is compared to the performance of other students of the same age or grade.

Metropolitan Achievement Tests—Reading
Gray Oral Reading Tests, 3rd Ed.
Wide Range Achievement Tests
Decoding Skills Test
WRMT Word Attack
Comprehensive Tests of Phonological Processing (CTOPP)

SB-4-Memory for Sentences
Verbal Selective
    Reminding Test
Rapid Automatized
    Naming Test
Boston Naming Test
Children's Auditory Verbal
    Learning Test–2
Wide Range Assessment of
    Memory and Learning
    (Story Memory)

> **These test specific abilities you need in order to learn and remember what you have learned. They evaluate your functioning in different areas of memory (e.g., long term vs. short term, visual vs. auditory).**

Rey Osterrieth Complex
    Figure
Beery Test of Visual Motor
    Integration

> **These give information about how well you understand, organize, and can reproduce what you see.**

IDENTIFYING INFORMATION

Stanley is a 16-year-old adolescent currently living in Dullsville with his parents and older brother. He attends the 10th grade at Dullsville High School where he receives special education services daily to help him complete the written language requirement for his classes.

Stanley has a history of Executive Function Disorder and Attention Deficit Hyperactivity Disorder for which he is taking a daily dose of Ritalin. These disabilities make it difficult for him to organize his thoughts and put them on paper to fulfill the written requirements for his social studies and English classes. Stanley particularly enjoys the math and science courses and is able to complete the work for those classes as there is less written work required.

Stanley was previously tested through the Dullsville School Department when he was in 7th grade. Past testing revealed that Stanley's intellectual functioning is in the high average range of ability.

BEHAVIORAL OBSERVATIONS

Stanley came to the testing situation willingly and rapport was established easily. He appeared to be aware of the difficulties he is having in school and was open to talking about them. He was interested in all of the test materials displayed

> This is important information because it tells parents and teachers how reliable the tests were. It does not mean "Big Brother" is watching you.

and needed to be continually redirected to focus on the task at hand. When focused, he demonstrated considerable effort on tasks. The first session was completed in about two hours with one short break. The second session was also about two hours.

There was no observable difference in his performance between the two days.

COGNITIVE TESTING

On the **WISC-III,** Stanley's scores fell solidly within the high average to superior range of intelligence. A comparison of his verbal versus his nonverbal performance scores shows that Stanley's nonverbal problem-solving skills are slightly stronger than his verbal comprehension and expressive language abilities.

This may be why math and sciences are easier than the written language performance in English and social studies.

There is a scatter in the testing which indicates that Stanley has several areas of relative strength and weakness.

Stanley's testing revealed excellent cognitive abilities. He has a good fund of general information, a good vocabulary, and strong reasoning skills in the area of arithmetic. This suggests that he is learning and retaining information that he is taught. He answered questions clearly and succinctly and his thoughts were well organized and logical. Stanley also has a well-developed ability for abstract concept formation. On the similarities subtest, he could express how two objects and abstract concepts were alike. He showed excellent verbal rea-

A scatter means that some of the scores on the different subtests within the main categories were above average and some of them were below average. Solid average for a subtest score is 10.

soning skills and could answer questions about social norms and conventions. His ability was equal whether information was concrete, more abstract, or inferential.

Stanley also displayed well-developed nonverbal, visual-spatial skills. He was especially capable with problem solving when provided with structure or a model. He used strategies appropriately and successfully.

> This part of the test involves putting puzzles together, copying block designs, attending to abstract details, and reading social cues in pictures.

On the **Rey Osterrieth Complex Figure** test, Stanley was highly skilled at copying the complex figure. He had an appreciation for the whole and the parts. He was also able to remember the drawing accurately over time. This showed good perceptual organization skills.

Stanley demonstrated variable rote memory skills. On the **Children's Auditory Verbal Learning Test–2** he had a good memory for the list of words. However, on the **Wide Range**

> Rote memory is what you can tell back that doesn't involve thinking, like a phone number.

Assessment of Memory and Learning, he could remember the general stories and most of the details, but he left out a number of the important details after a period of time. This compromised

> This may be why he is having difficulty when taking notes and when studying for tests. He may need someone to show him how new information relates to previously learned information and he may need frequent review to help him remember.

his ability to answer questions about the stories. This indicates that he may not have good strategies for processing and retaining more complex verbal information.

RECEPTIVE LANGUAGE SKILLS

The **Peabody Picture Vocabulary Test (PPVT-III)** was given to assess Stanley's ability to recognize single word vocabulary items. He was asked to point to a named picture from a field of four pictures. He did well on this test and received a score that placed him at the 77th percentile.

Percentile allows us to measure an individual's performance compared to that of the normative population. This means that if 100 students were given this test, he did better than 76 of them. This is not the same as a 77 on a test. The 77th percentile is a very good score. The 50th percentile is exactly average.

On the receptive language portion of the **Clinical Evaluation of Language Fundamentals (CELF-3)**, Stanley showed a good understanding of the concepts. He received an average score of 100 that placed him at the 50th percentile. He did the best on the *Concepts and Directions* subtest. He missed only a few of the details and showed a good understanding of the concepts. This shows that he can follow oral directions at an age-appropriate level. He had an average score on the word association subtest and also showed average ability in understanding various semantic relationships expressed in sentences. On the *Listening to Paragraphs* subtest he received a score of 8 that placed him at the 25th percentile. This subtest measured his ability to recall longer and more complex information.

EXPRESSIVE LANGUAGE SKILLS

The **Beery Picture Vocabulary Test** was used to assess Stanley's expressive language skills. He received a score of 100 that placed him at the 50th percentile that shows an average ability to understand and use vocabulary. He exhibited some long pauses when he tried to recall words. Often, he would name the function of the pictured items rather than the exact word. This could be an indication of a word retrieval problem.

On the expressive language portion of the **Clinical Evaluation of Language Fundamentals (CELF-3)**, he received a standard score of 116 that placed him at the 86th percentile. The results of these subtests indicated average short-term auditory memory skills, good ability to create compound and complex sentences, and a superior ability to formulate grammatical sentences.

ACADEMIC TESTING

On the **Woodcock-Johnson Reading Assessment** Stanley's

Many of us have word retrieval problems at some time. When you can't remember the name of a film you just saw or a song you love, you are having difficulty retrieving the information. Usually, if you give yourself some time, you come up with that name and the momentary lapse doesn't bother you or your conversation. If you are having this difficulty often, it can present problems at school. You might have difficulty remembering the parts of a sentence or the state capitals or chemistry elements. If this is the case, you will need to learn some strategies to help you with your schoolwork, so it is important to identify the problem.

Broad Reading score was in the average range. There was some variability in the components of the assessment. On the *Word Identification* subtest (16th percentile), he made a few careless errors and his mistakes were close visually to the test words ("knew" for "know" and "island" for "inland"). Stanley clearly had learned decoding strategies but he struggled using them with multisyllabic regular and irregular words. He slowly pronounced the words syllable by syllable but could not always hear the word in totality. Similarly, on the *Word Attack* subtest, he scored in the low average range (20th percentile) and he often guessed at the overall look of a word. He had the most difficulty with vowel sounds and vowel combinations.

Stanley's score on the *Passage Comprehension* subtest was well within the average range (47th percentile). On this test, he was required to silently read a short passage and supply a missing word. As the passages became more difficult, he was slow and methodical. In many cases, even though he made errors, his answers showed an understanding of the paragraph.

On the *Reading Vocabulary* portion, Stanley was required to read a word and come up with an appropriate antonym or synonym. He also scored within the average range on this subtest (44th percentile). Due to his well-developed vocabulary skills, he might have scored higher on this test. However, he was not always able to correctly decode the target word so he could not produce the correct antonym or synonym.

Based on this assessment, it appears that Stanley continues to struggle with decoding. The Basic Reading score (18th percentile) is a combination of comprehension and decoding. This score places him at a 4th grade instructional reading level. He has a good vocabulary and is able to use the context clues of a paragraph to help him with meaning. However, he needs to exert so much effort to decode that his understanding and memory for more lengthy passages is compromised.

On the **Woodcock-Johnson Math Assessment**, Stanley's scores were solidly in the average range throughout the subtests. He was focused and worked diligently throughout this portion of the assessment. He was able to perform multistep calculations and to use multiplication, division, and decimals. The mistakes he made were careless, such as adding when he should have subtracted. On the *Calculation* subtest, he scored at the 61st percentile.

On the *Applied Problems* subtest, he scored at the 55th percentile. This section involved mathematical reasoning, problem solving, and applications. Errors on this section were due to impulsivity and carelessness that might have been avoided if he had used the scrap paper provided.

On the **Woodcock-Johnson Written Language Assessment**, Stanley's scores were at a mid–3rd grade level. This score is composed of dictation and a writing sample. The *Dictation* portion required written responses that measured punctuation, capitalization, spelling, and word usage. The majority of his errors were in spelling. There were minor errors of punctuation, such as forgetting the comma between a city and a state and not capitalizing proper nouns.

The *Writing Samples* subtest measured his ability to write for different purposes. Stanley's sentences were detailed and the paragraph was clear, complete, and well organized. Again, he had difficulty with spelling, although he was not penalized for spelling errors for this portion of the assessment. Although the test was untimed, his difficulty with spelling clearly slowed him down. This has significant implications for classroom writing activities and open-response testing situations. His poor decoding skills make the mechanics of writing laborious.

On the **Woodcock-Johnson Knowledge Assessment**, Stanley scored in the average range (50th percentile). Stanley appeared to enjoy this section of the test and was fully engaged in the tasks. He responded to most items with little hesitation. On the *Science* portion, he had few mistakes on his answers to general knowledge questions of biology and physical science (50th percentile). On the *Social Studies* section, his knowledge was adequate (37th percentile) about history, geography, government, and home and community awareness. The *Humanities* section tests knowledge of art, music, and literature. Stanley scored in the average range (40th percentile) in this area also. These scores indicate that he is able to learn information through listening, watching, thinking, and reading.

SOCIAL AND EMOTIONAL FUNCTIONING

Stanley presents as a sensitive, friendly teenager with the typical interests of a 16-year-old boy. He reported that he likes to spend time with his friends, listening to music, and snowboarding in the winter. He appears to enjoy his relationship with his parents and with his older brother when his brother is home on vacation from college.

Stanley's responses to questions indicated that he is happy more than he is sad, although he appears to be sad. Testing also indicated that he has sad and lonely feelings. On the ***Achenbach Youth Self Report*** he endorsed items which suggest that he feels tired and sad. He appears very much aware of his academic problems and his frustration with his reading and writing seems to overshadow his many strengths and contribute to his feelings of sadness and loneliness.

> Remember, these are the qualitative answers where the examiner is looking at the quality of what Stanley says and draws conclusions about his answers to questions.

SUMMARY

In summary, Stanley is a bright young man who has strong verbal comprehension and reasoning ability. His strengths are his nonverbal, visual-spatial skills. His short-term memory for short units of information is solid. His areas of difficulty are in remembering more complex and detailed information. He has some difficulty in the classroom with attention and organization. He continues to meet the classification of Executive Function Disability with Attention Deficit Hyperactivity Disorder.

> Many states require the label of a disability in order to provide special education services. This designation allows the services and determines the type of help you will get in school. It is not a stamp on your forehead but the key to services.

Language testing indicated average to superior language skills with some difficulties noted in word retrieval.

On academic testing, there was a significant discrepancy in his *Broad Written Language* score that is influenced by Stanley's poor ability to automatically identify correct sound/symbol relationships in words. Stanley has difficulty with reading and decoding and does not like to read. His reading difficulties affect his ability to read grade level material and to gain skills in other areas.

RECOMMENDATIONS

1. No language services are recommended at this time.

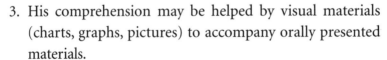

This is the part where they tell you what they are going to do to help you.

2. He may need extra time to participate in class discussions due to his word retrieval difficulties.

3. His comprehension may be helped by visual materials (charts, graphs, pictures) to accompany orally presented materials.

4. His parents are encouraged to consult with Stanley's pediatrician about his continued attention issues to determine if the medication dosage is adequate.

5. Because Stanley may have difficulty organizing complex or lengthy information, he should be encouraged to ask his teachers for extra help when he is unsure what to do.

6. Assignments need to be broken down into smaller units and he should clearly understand the tasks involved before beginning the assignment. He may need help determining

the order of the steps involved and with setting up and beginning the task.

7. Stanley should have access to Books on Tape for his classroom work as well as for recreational books.

8. Stanley should have access to a computer with spell check for lengthy written assignments.

9. It might be helpful for Stanley to use a tape recorder for dictating lengthy written assignments as well.

SAMPLE TEST SCORES

Wechsler Intelligence Scale for Children—3rd Ed. (WISC-III)

Verbal Subtest	Scaled Score	Nonverbal Subtest	Scaled Score
Information	11	Picture Completion	14
Similarities	11	Coding	12
Arithmetic	12	Picture Arrangement	15
Vocabulary	11	Block Design	14
Comprehension	16	Object Assembly	10

Full Scale IQ	118
Verbal IQ	113
Nonverbal IQ	120

Scaled Scores are scores that have been statistically transformed to have a specific mean and standard deviation. This allows us to compare the scores to other students at the same age and grade and to convert it to a percentile.

The following are other ways to indicate test scores:

✳ *Mean*   The average score obtained by a population that is given a particular test.

✳ *Standard Deviation*   A measure of the extent of which a score varies from the mean. For example, a score over 1.5 standard

Clinical Evaluation of Language Fundamentals (CELF-3)

Subtest	Scaled Score	Percentile
Expressive Language		
Concepts and Directions	11	63
Word Classes	10	50
Semantic Relationships	09	37
Receptive Language		
Formulated Sentences	13	84
Recalling Sentences	11	63
Sentence Assembly	14	91
Listening to Paragraphs	08	25

deviations from the mean might be needed in some states to determine if a student has a learning disability.

✳ *Stanine* Like a scaled score, but using a single digit scoring system from 1 to 5.

✳ *Age-equivalent* The average score obtained on a test by children of various ages.

✳ *Grade-equivalent* The average score obtained on a test by children in various grades. This is not an indication that a person has the same skills as a student of that grade. For example, a grade score of 4th grade means that Stanley got the same number of questions right as a typical student at the beginning of 4th grade. He may or may not have the same skills as the typical 4th grader.

✳ *Percentiles* A score that indicates its rank, as compared to others of the same age or grade. For most tests, 25th–75th percentile is considered average.

What Does It All Mean?

What do we know now that we didn't know before? We know how Stanley learns best. We know what type of help and technical accommodations he needs in order to be more successful in the classroom. We know how he compares with other students in his grade in his academic areas and in his receptive and expressive language skills. We also know that he continues to need special education services, where those services should focus, and where they should be delivered. We also know that Stanley is affected by his difficulties in reading and written language and he will need help in dealing with the frustration of his disability.

You must be careful about reading too much into your test scores, however. A score is only an indication of how you did on a particular day at a particular time. Your answers to the test questions were dependent upon your knowledge as well as how much sleep you had the night before, how you were feeling about your friends and yourself on that day, the temperature in the room, the noise outside the room, and many other factors. Test scores alone should never be the only way of making educational decisions. In Stanley's case, the scores were used in conjunction with medical opinions about his ADHD and with teacher reports about his work in class.

Because Stanley is having such difficulty with reading and written language, and because that difficulty is due to his organization and attention disabilities, he is eligible for special education services to continue. Without the testing, it would not be possible to be as certain about Stanley's need for services. Students, especially at the high school level, fail to succeed for many different reasons. Problems at home, problems with social life, drugs, alcohol, bad teacher/student match, illness, and truancy are just some of the other reasons why students have difficulty in school. These reasons may not make them eligible for special education services. The documentation of Stanley's learning disability and his difficulty in school are what makes him eligible to receive the special help.

The IEP

Dialogues—What You Might Say

This chapter discusses your involvement in your Individualized Education Plan (IEP). Because you will have to be actively involved in your plan, it is important that you know what to say. You may feel awkward talking about your learning disability or you may not know how to ask for what you need. To help you along, we have scattered sample dialogues (things you might say) throughout this chapter to help guide you in forming your own comments. You will need to alter them to make them fit your circumstances, but they can be useful as a general guide. The dialogues are written in italics; *the print looks like this.*

What an IEP Is and Why You Need to Know about It

I would like to read my IEP. I believe it will help me understand my learning disability and it will help me understand what is expected of me. I can tell you a lot about my problems in the classroom, so I would like to be involved in my next IEP meeting.

If you are a student with a learning disability and you are receiving special education services at your school, you have an Individualized Education Plan (IEP). If you are like most high school students with learning disabilities, you have probably never seen it. Many don't even know they have one. According to recent research, that's a big problem. Why? Because students who are directly involved with creating their learning plans have the greatest success in high school and in college.

Knowing that, you probably want to know more about this learning plan. What is an IEP and what does it have to do with your life? An IEP is a plan of action for you and for your teachers and it is designed to help you succeed. This written document describes your learning disability, the skills you need to work on, and what services and/or assistive technologies the school will provide to help you meet your goals. As we mention in the special section on rights in chapter 12, your school must provide a plan written just for you. The plan outlines strategies or accommodations teachers are expected to provide.

Up until now, your parents have probably helped design your plan. Because your parents are so concerned about your success, it is not surprising that they have been involved. They are strong supporters and work hard to see that school meets your needs. Many parents, however, don't realize how important it is for their children to be involved too. If you have been telling your parents you want to make more decisions and want to have more control over your life, here is a perfect opportunity to show them you are ready to be treated like a young adult.

> Try to attend the IEP meetings; these can help when you get stuck in a situation where a teacher could question you, and you can point out to them that it is on your IEP.
> —Molly Gonzalez, a recent college grad with learning disabilities

Your involvement in your educational plan can make the difference between success and failure. When you add your thoughts, experiences, and opinions to your educational plan, you become a part of the team. After all, the plan is intended to help you.

Before you can contribute to your plan, you need to understand the IEP and the process that is involved in creating it. Each year a team sits down to discuss your strengths and weaknesses and comes up with educational goals for the year. The team might include a regular classroom teacher, your special education teacher, your guidance counselor, your parents, and other people from the special education office. If you are sixteen, you *must* be invited to these meetings. If you are younger, you may ask to be involved too.

If you believe you are ready to help create your plan, you need to be prepared. Ask your special education teacher or your parent when your next IEP meeting will be held and tell them you want to attend. If you don't know what to say, use the sample dialogue at the beginning of this chapter. You should allow yourself at least a few weeks to get ready for the meeting. Most often meetings are held during the school year when you have a lot of other work to do. Getting ready for the meeting takes time and you will want to have enough information to understand what is going on.

Understanding Your Disability

First, you need to know the name of your learning disability. Maybe you have heard your parents say you have ADHD or dyslexia or a nonverbal learning disability. You probably know you have a problem, but you might not know the specific name of your disorder. Ask your special education teacher to define your learning disability for you. She might be surprised when you ask. Have her describe it in a way you can understand. Most special educators have lots of practice in explaining learning disabilities and are pleased when students take an interest. An explanation of many learning disabilities is available in chapter 1 and explanations of specific disabilities are found in chapters 3 through 8. Students with specific disabilities might say:

I have dyslexia. I have trouble understanding what I read. I have a hard time doing my social studies homework when I have to remember what I read.

I have ADHD. It makes it hard for me to sit still during class. I find it especially hard to listen when teachers just talk.

I have dysgraphia. I have trouble writing. It takes me much longer to write than most students.

Once you have heard and understood the definition of your disability, think about what it means to you. How does it affect your schoolwork? Make a list of areas where you believe your learning disability creates problems. If you have trouble writing, ask your special educa-tion teacher or your parents to help you with your list. Practice talking about your disability and the problems it creates. If you had a broken hand, you wouldn't have trouble explaining that tying your shoes is hard. Using the examples above, practice describing the ways your learning disability affects your schoolwork and your relationships with your teachers and your classmates. It's not always easy to talk about the things that give us trouble, but if you can say what your problem is and how it affects your learning, that means you understand your learning disability and you are ready to contribute to your IEP.

If you are taking medicine to help you in school, be sure you know what the medicine is called and how it helps. If your medicine has side effects that may interfere with your schoolwork, be sure you can describe your symptoms.

Read Your Current IEP

Once you understand what your learning disability is, you are ready to read your current IEP. Tell your teacher or your parents you want to be involved in the next IEP meeting and that you need to read your current IEP to help you get ready. Again, they may be surprised when you ask to see your plan. Sometimes teachers and parents believe stu-dents will be hurt by what they read. We believe you are old enough to read this report. It is, after all, your abilities and disabilities that it describes. You may not agree with everything you read.

I don't understand this section of the IEP. Can you explain this to me?

Reading IEPs can seem overwhelming at first, especially for those with trouble reading, but don't be discouraged. Some of the terms are difficult for most people to understand. People who work with special education have expressions they like to use to describe

SECTIONS OF THE IEP

By law, your IEP must include certain information about you. This information is usually organized into the sections listed below. When you look at your current IEP, you will probably see these sections or information. The new IEP you help develop will also have these sections or information:

- Current levels of educational performance: This section includes precise information about how you are doing in school and sometimes in other aspects of your life

- What special education and related services the school will provide for you

- How much of your school day will be spent in regular education classrooms

- Goals for the year

- Short-term objectives (the individual steps that make up the annual goals)

- When the school will start providing services to you and how long the services are expected to last

- How the school will find out if you are accomplishing the goals and objectives set for you (called "evaluation criteria")

- Assistive technology devices (such as a computer or communication board) the school will provide to help you. IEP team members are required to consider assistive technology as an option.

- Transition services you need to get ready for life after finishing high school

NICHCY - National Information Center for Children and Youth with Disabilities learning and teaching styles. They work with these words every day and are comfortable with them. Just like baseball fans know what an ERA is and movie fans know what a DVD is, you will come to understand the terms associated with your learning style. You may need to ask your parents or a teacher to explain some of them, or you can look in the glossary section of this book. If you ask, your special education teacher can explain the different sections of IEPs to give you an understanding of how they are organized. See the chart outlining sections of the IEP.

Your plan may have some surprises in it. Since most students have never been involved in their IEPs, many are surprised and sometimes discouraged when they read some of the things the document says about them. When you read your plan, you may be surprised by some of the things it says about you. You may agree with what it says. You may not. In either case, it is important that you know what it says. If you don't agree with the plan or what it says, don't get angry. You now have an opportunity to contribute to your plan and to suggest changes in the areas you believe need to be changed.

Moving Forward

Once you have read your current IEP, begin to think about your strengths and weaknesses. We all do some things better than others. The number one student in your class may not be able to program his VCR. The star on your school's soccer team may not be able to dance. Ask yourself: What am I good at? What do I enjoy doing? Which classes do I really like? Why do I like those classes?

Then think about the areas that are not as easy. Ask yourself: Which class is hardest for me? Why does it give me so much trouble? What could make this class easier for me? Would it help if I used a tape recorder in the classroom? Would it be easier if I used a computer for my notes? Could I use more time for my tests, or have an extra textbook at home that I could use? Maybe you are a slow starter in the morning. Many high school students are. Maybe it would be better if that class that gives you trouble were later in the day—maybe just the opposite. Maybe you learn best first thing in the morning. In that case, it might be better for you to have your most difficult class first. You probably know better than anyone else does what makes the class hard and what would make it easier. Try to come up with some suggestions or "accommodations" that would make schoolwork less difficult.

Sometimes personalities or teaching styles affect learning. Think about the teachers you like. What makes those teachers special? Then, think about the teacher you dread. What makes you think that teacher is a jerk? (Of course, you wouldn't call the teacher a jerk in a meeting, but you might be able to explain why the teacher's style isn't helpful.)

What are your goals for the future? Answers to these questions will help you set your goals. Maybe you are having trouble with algebra. Maybe you don't understand your world studies textbook. Maybe writing essays is hard for you. Think about those areas that have given you trouble in the past and that you would like to feel better about at the end of the year. A short-term goal might be that you would pass math this year. That goal may contribute to a more long-term goal, graduation from high school, for example. You may be thinking of going on to college, or you may have a particular job in mind. Think about what you would like to be able to do at the end of this year and what you would like to be ready for when you graduate.

All of this thinking will help you develop ideas for your new IEP and for the statement of transition services that we will cover in the next chapter.

Practice What to Say

I have been thinking about the way I learn. I have thought about the things I do really well and the things I need to work on. I have also been thinking about what I really want to do this year. I would like to tell you what I think.

Once you have thought about yourself, the way you learn, your strengths and weaknesses, things that make learning easier, and so forth, make some notes or lists. Include the information you have been thinking about—a list of strengths and areas than need work, classes you find easy, classes you find difficult, things you think may help you learn, and so on. Once you have your notes ready, practice what you would like to say at the IEP meeting. Your special education teacher will probably be willing to help you with this. If not, you can practice with your parents or on your own.

Practice telling yourself that you have always been great at helping little kids or that you are the best computer repair person in the school or that you can design your own clothes. Don't be afraid to talk about the things you enjoy and those you do well. Then, practice talking about the things that are hard for you. Acknowledge that you don't do your homework, or that you just can't read the textbook, or that you feel it is impossible to read or talk in front of the class. Then talk about the things you think could make learning easier and what your goals are. Practice will really help you when you get to your meeting and share your thoughts with the people there. You will know what you want to say and you will know how to say it.

If the date of your IEP meeting has already been set, let your special education teacher know that you are ready. If it hasn't already been set, ask your special education teacher to schedule it as soon as possible. Use all the time before the meeting practicing what you want to say.

Meeting Day

I don't think that's how I am. I can sit still when the subject is interesting and when I can understand what is going on. . . . I agree it would be easier to pay attention if the teacher stopped at my desk as he walked around the room.

You are ready. You've given lots of thought to the way you learn and you want to share what you know with others who care about your success. Your teachers, your parents, and your counselors are sure to be impressed with all you have done. You are now a full member of the team. Ask if you can speak first. When you go first, you will be the first to mention your learning disability and the areas that you find difficult. That way you won't have to hear it from somebody else. You will have suggestions for helping yourself pay attention. You will feel the power of helping yourself.

Once you have presented your thoughts, listen to what the others have to say. There will probably be a few things you haven't thought of or other suggestions for accommodations. You may not agree with all of the comments, but it is unusual for any group of people to agree about everything. While other people are speaking, take notes and write down your questions. Try not to interrupt, but if you must say something be sure to say, "excuse me" and let the speaker finish his thought.

If you have had evaluations recently, the results of those tests may be discussed. If this is the first time you have heard the results, listen and take notes. If you don't agree, that's okay. Let the team know you don't necessarily agree with the results of the tests. Tests only measure what you did on that day at that time. (Explanations of tests can be found in chapter 9.)

Try to agree on the way your teachers will grade you, or evaluate you, on your success. Will it be considered a success if you get a C on your next English essay, or will you have met your goal if you pass French?

During the meeting, make eye contact. Smile. Be polite. Be ready to accept praise. Don't be afraid to ask questions or to ask members of the team to restate comments in language that you understand. As we mentioned earlier, special educators sometimes have their own language. You should not be expected to understand it.

Your teachers, counselors, and parents are going to see what a great job you have done and will recognize that you are now a young adult ready to be involved in your own educational planning. Once the meeting is over, go over your new IEP. You should understand all of it now, but if there are any areas that are still unclear, be sure to ask your teacher or your parents to explain them. You spent a lot of time making the IEP just right for you, so look at it during the year and work hard on the areas you felt needed work. When you have accomplished one or all of the goals on your plan, ask for a new meeting to set new goals.

Older students must have a transition component to IEPs. This is the part of the plan that will help you get ready for your life after high school graduation. If this applies to you, check out the next chapter.

REMEMBER

- Successful students are involved in IEP meetings.
- You are the most important member of the IEP team.
- You need to understand your disability in order to participate.
- You must be invited to the meetings if you are sixteen or older; you may be involved if you are younger.
- Don't expect to understand everything on your IEP the first time you read it. Ask for explanations.
- You need to practice what you will say at meetings.
- You need to set goals and help develop a plan to help you meet those goals.

Resources

Learning Disabilities Association of America (LDA)
   4156 Library Road
   Pittsburgh, PA 15234
   (412) 341-1515
   http://www.ldanatl.org/

The National Information Center for Children and Youth
with Disabilities (NICHCY)
   P. O. Box 1492
   Washington, DC 20013
   (800) 695-0285
   http://www.nichcy.org

Transition Planning

Definition—What Is a Transition?

Because some high schools refer to programs directed at life-skills activities for students with mental retardation as "transitional" programs, many students with learning disabilities are confused and upset when they hear the term applied to them. The dictionary defines *transition* as a "passage from one form, state, style, or place to another." For the purposes of this chapter, the "transition" period is the passage from high school to life after high school, or the time you spend preparing for what you will do after high school graduation. For most students, the transition period should begin in their freshman year. Some may have the flexibility of waiting a little longer. But, for all students, the sooner they begin to think about life after high school, the better.

The frustration and anxiety associated with learning for students with disabilities often makes them want to forget any further education after high school. If you have found your educational time in high school unpleasant, you may fall into this category. Remember, however, that high school is not always the best educational place for students with learning disabilities. Educational opportunities after high school can often focus on your areas of strength. Perhaps the support services you needed weren't available in high school. Today, many colleges offer solid support systems for students with a variety of learning disabilities. Although the college's level of responsibility is very different from the responsibilities of public high schools, the accommodations and assistive technologies they provide can often be just what learning disabled students need to excel. Recent research confirms that students with learning disabilities can succeed in college, yet many students are not encouraged, assisted, or prepared to go. Your involvement during this time of transition can overcome all three deterrents.

Some students are more interested in direct career preparation. For them, the transition from high school to a vocational school or a community college may be the most appropriate. If direct preparation for a job you love is what you want, this type of educational experience may be right for you.

Some students are interested in the military as a post–high school option. For many, the structure of military training makes it the right choice. Still other students are eager to enter the workforce immediately without further education. No matter what you have in mind, it is important that you begin to think about these things now. That doesn't mean you need to make a lifelong decision in your freshman year in high school, it just means you need to be thinking about it. Preparation for some post–high school options begins earlier than others, so you need to start considering what you want to do after high school.

The Transitional Plan

The previous chapter provided information about the importance of IEPs and especially your involvement in the IEP process. An IEP is the Individualized Educational Plan designed specifically for you. You should be involved in all IEP planning, and once you reach high school, that involvement is not only suggested, it is mandated. If you are over sixteen, you must be involved in your educational plan. A specific part of the IEP, "the Transitional Plan," sometimes called Transitional IEP (TIEP) or Individualized Transition Plan (ITP), focuses on your post–high school goals and the skills and programs you will need to meet your goals. In a recent article in the *Journal of Learning Disabilities*, Loring C. Brinckerhoff called this time "a golden opportunity for students." Whether you are interested in college, vocational school, the military, or the world of work, your transition team will help you prepare to make the move from high school to the world of adulthood.

> Individualized transition planning should be viewed as a golden opportunity for students to shape their own academic destinies by learning about their disabilities, asking questions, presenting ideas, and advocating for themselves.
>
> —Loring C. Brinckerhoff

The Transition Team

As with the traditional IEP, the members of your transition team will include you, your parents, your special education teachers, and perhaps a regular classroom teacher, a guidance counselor, a psychologist, or other educational specialist. The team might also call upon other professionals to help you meet your goals. These members of the team might act as consultants and may not come to all meetings, but instead be involved on a one-time basis. Depending on your strengths, disabilities, and especially your goals, consultants may also include community representatives from mental health agencies, independent living centers, and/or the social security administration. Because transitional plans are created for *all* students with disabilities, not just learning disabilities, a wide variety of community services can be accessed while creating transitional IEPs. For students with learning disabilities, these agencies might provide vocational guidance, college training opportunities, mentorship programs, work incentive programs, and so forth. Your high school's special education department can help you determine whether you qualify for the services these agencies provide. In addition to these community service agencies, consultants could include representatives from colleges or trade schools, job service agencies from the Department of Labor, and even individual employers who might provide training.

Depending on your strengths, your learning disability, and your goals, you and your transition team will consider:

✳ postsecondary education
✳ vocational training
✳ employment
✳ independent living
✳ community participation

The most important member of the transition team is you. You set the goals that drive the plan. Now, more than ever, what you think and want will drive your education and influence which high school courses you choose to take.

Developing the Plan

The National Information Center for Children and Youth with Disabilities (NICHY) presents five areas that you and your transition team must consider when developing and implementing your transitional plan.

1. Assessment

This part of the transition plan considers what it is you want and identifies your strengths and weaknesses as they relate to your goals. Your team should be considering what you like to do, the type of work that might be best for you, and where in the community you will find success. You need to be ready to tell the team about your hopes and dreams. Do you want to go to college, to vocational school, into the service, or directly to work? Do you want to take a year to explore by volunteering or participating in an alternative form of education? Of course, your parents will help you consider your options and will be involved in helping you set your goals. Once you have decided your direction, the team will begin to assess your skills. They might review your academic standing, your test scores, and your course work, and they may recommend additional tests. In fact, you will need up-to-date diagnostic tests to receive accommodations in college. You may choose to get retested now, or you may request an exit evaluation (including a new psychological assessment) to provide current information required for accommodations at college. They will assess your social skills and help you determine whether you are ready to pursue your goals immediately after high school or whether you will need further skill development. Your assistive technology needs should also be considered at this time.

The team should discuss the type of educational setting or vocational setting you are interested in. For example, is your goal to go to an Ivy League or very competitive college? Are you interested in a less competitive state school? Do you want to live at home and go to a community college? What career plans do you have after college? If you aren't interested in going to college right now, are you interested in the National Guard or the Air Force? You will want to be ready to discuss these kinds of options. You should be ready to discuss whether you learn best alone or in groups, whether you learn best by watching, reading, or listening. The team will discuss the types of supports you will need to help prepare for the area you choose.

If you are a high school athlete and plan to play a sport in college, there are specific NCAA eligibility requirements. Contacts with the NCAA should be included in your transition plan.

2. Development

The second piece of the Transitional IEP involves the development of options. If your goal is to go to college, these might include visiting colleges, attending a college night, meeting with LD peers who are now in college, researching colleges (see chapter 14), and discussing financial issues. If you are interested in going to work, the development portion of the IEP may include finding a volunteer job in the area of your choice, involvement in an internship program, job shadowing, or similar opportunities. You should be looking at want ads to help you become better aware of the job market. The team may want to contact employers or community program representatives who might provide information, and identify community programs that offer job placement services. The team should pull together your records, including current documentation of your learning disability. You should have a copy of all your records when you leave school.

3. Matching

The third part of transitional planning is making a match. This is when you and your team will discuss your college choices and analyze the requirements for acceptance, the services they provide, the housing opportunities, and so on. For those going to work, the team will consider the demands and expectations of individual jobs. They will review duties, skills, wages, benefits, and similar aspects of the job. They will identify the gaps in your education that need to be remedied.

4. Preparation and Training

Your team will help you identify the required course work you will need to be considered at your postsecondary choice, and they will help you identify the support you will need to succeed in those courses. They can help you identify the accommodations you will need in the college setting. If you need to improve your learning skills and work on new strategies, study skills should be a part of your academic program now.

The team can help you with your applications, your interviews, and the test preparations you may need. For career oriented students, the team can provide instruction on job-seeking skills and they can identify community-based work experiences, and potential service providers. They can also help identify accommodations you may need on the job.

Because students won't have a transitional team to help them succeed after high school, self-advocacy training should be a part of any high school student's transitional plan. Being a part of your transition team can be the first step in acquiring the self-advocacy skills you will need to succeed as an adult. See more about this below.

5. Placement and Follow-Up

The team may help monitor progress once the student is in the desired setting. They may be able to make suggestions and recommendations and/or act as advocates if the student needs help.

Self-Advocacy

Since you will be a part of your transition team, you need to begin your preparations now. If you want to go to a four-year college, there may be specific academic courses you are required to take. If you want to go into the military, there may be specific requirements you need to address. If you want to go to work, you want to have the skills you need for the job you will love when you graduate. If you want to take a year to explore alternatives, you need a

> Many [students] do not understand the way their strengths relate to the way they learn.... To be able to say I am really good when I hear things because I have a good memory for what I hear, or when I see things I can analyze them ... that is the kind of information students need to have.
>
> —Lisa Ijiri,
> director for Advancement
> of Learning, Curry College

> People are more appreciative if you're honest.... Say "I need to write that down."
>
> —Laura,
> a third-year college student

> My best advice is to know what you can do. It takes me ten minutes to read five pages. When you're assigned work, you know how much time you need to leave yourself.
>
> —Eric,
> a college freshman

plan. You need to start getting ready. In order to participate in your transition team meetings and to find success after high school you need to become a self-advocate. You need to be able to take on the responsibilities of a young adult. The following will help you achieve that goal:

* Write down your long-term goals and include a list of the things you need to do to meet those goals.

* Review your IEP and your transitional plan and decide if the plan is being implemented and if any changes need to be made to help you reach your goals.

* Be involved in all IEP meetings and transitional team meetings. Learn about your disability and be able to explain it to someone else, including the academic and social challenges of your specific disability.

* Learn to present a positive self-image by explaining your areas of strength.

* Learn and use study and organizational skills and strategies and be able to explain which ones work best for you.

* Learn to identify and to access the special education services that are available at your school.

* Learn about your civil rights under the law (see chapter 12) and be able to explain the laws to someone else.

* Learn to ask for the specific accommodations that you need to succeed.

* Practice interviewing, whether for college admission or for work. Practice making eye contact, expressing yourself clearly (no slang), listening without interrupting, and asking questions.

* Select high school courses that will help you meet your post–high school goals.

✳ Talk to your doctor and/or psychologist. Have them explain the results of your tests in a way that you understand. If you are taking medications, be sure you know what you are taking and why.

✳ Get a job. Not all students can handle academics and work, but even a part-time job can improve your financial situation and your self-esteem. Employment can help you with organization, money management, career exploration, and prioritization. Plan how you will spend or save your earnings.

✳ Open a checking account and learn to use it.

✳ Prepare meals for your family. Plan, shop, and prepare meals. Once you leave high school, you will need to be more self-sufficient. You may have a meal plan at college that will provide most of your meals, but you should know how to shop and to cook.

✳ Do your own laundry. Unless you plan to FedEx your dirty clothes home to Mom, you had better learn how to do your own laundry. It is better to make the mistake of washing a red shirt with your underwear while you are still living at home. Pink underwear can be embarrassing at college.

✳ Join an extracurricular group and take a leadership position. Again, not all students can juggle schoolwork and extracurriculars, but involvement in a volunteer organization, a club, or athletic team can help you with leadership and social skills.

Your involvement in your transitional team will help you develop self-advocacy skills and will put you in an excellent position to begin reaching for your goals. More specific information about college, career, and the military is included in the next chapters.

Resources

HEATH Resource Center
   One Dupont Circle, Suite 800
   Washington, DC 20036-1193
   http://www.acenet.edu/Programs/HEATH/home.cfm

National Information Center for Children and Youth with
Disabilities (NICHCY)
   P. O. Box 1492
   Washington, DC 20013
   (800) 695-0285
   http://www.nichcy.org

The Law and Your Rights

A Clarification of Terms

One of the barriers to understanding special education legislation is the language involved. The terms *disability*, *mental impairments*, *mental illness*, *organic brain syndrome*, and *handicapping condition* are terms that most young people don't like to hear. Unfortunately, you don't get to choose the terms used by educators and legislators. While most young people think of *physical* disabilities when they hear the term *disabled* or *handicapped*, federal legislation includes learning disabilities when it uses that language. Though you may find the labels uncomfortable, these are the terms that must be used to identify your learning disability if you are to receive individualized programs or accommodations. In terms of the law, whether the problems come as a result of a physical disability, a mental illness, or specific learning disabilities, the law is the same. The laws are intended to prevent discrimination and to help provide a level playing field when those with disabilities go to school or to work. Try to get beyond the labels associated with these laws and focus on the kinds of positive differences these labels can make in your life.

A History of Special Education Legislation

The information in this section is provided for students who are curious about the history of special education. If you are interested, the following overview of disability and educational legislation will satisfy your curiosity. If you are more interested in how the current legislation affects you, jump ahead to the How the Law Affects Your Education section.

Laws supporting those with disabilities have a long history. Federal laws designed to help those with disabilities have been around since the late 1700s. The Public Health Service has its origins in a 1798 law that originally provided services to sick and disabled seamen. Since then, numerous laws have changed the way those with disabilities are treated and educated.

Until the 1960s, children with disabilities were often excluded from the public schools. Those who had physical disabilities were often educated in private institutional settings or they remained at home. Those with learning disabilities were often assumed to be dumb, lazy, or unmotivated, and sometimes they were even described as disruptive troublemakers. Some were called retarded or brain damaged, and, if they remained in public school, they were isolated from other students and given little opportunity for success. Many learning disabilities were unrecognized or unidentified, and often students were thrown out of school or failed to graduate. Some managed to make it through high school and some even made it to college, but most were scarred by their mistreatment and lack of success in school.

Starting in 1965, Congress began addressing the needs of students who had special educational needs. The information in this section is adapted from information provided by the National Information Center for Children and Youth with Disabilities.

The Elementary and Secondary Education Act of 1965 (ESEA) (P.L. 89-10):

✳ Addressed the educational opportunities for "economically underprivileged" children

✳ Provided the basis for special education legislation

The Elementary and Secondary Education Act Amendments of 1965 (ESEA) (P.L. 89-313):

✳ Authorized grants to state institutions and state-operated schools that served children with disabilities

---

HOW FEDERAL LAWS ARE MADE AND WHAT P.L. MEANS

When an Act is passed by Congress and signed into law by the president, it is given a number, such as P.L. 89-750. P.L. stands for Public Law. The first set of numbers means the session of Congress during which the law was passed. For example, the 89 means the 89th session of the U.S. Congress. The second number represents the number of the laws in the order they were passed.

P.L. 89-750 was the 750th law passed during the 89th congressional session.

These laws can be changed and amended.

Information provided by National Information Center for Children and Youth with Disabilities

✳ The first federal grant program specifically targeted for children and youth with disabilities

ESEA Amendments of 1966 (P.L. 89-750):

✳ Provided the first federal grants program designed to educate children in the public school setting

✳ The Bureau of Education of the Handicapped (BEH) and the National Advisory Council (now called the National Council on Disability) were also established at that time

ESEA Amendments of 1968 (P.L. 90-247):

✳ Established programs designed to supplement, support, and expand special education services (These programs were later called "discretionary.")

The Elementary and Secondary Education Act Amendments of 1970:

✳ Included Title VI, the Education of the Handicapped Act

✳ Established a grant program for local education agencies

Section 504 of the Rehabilitation Act of 1973 (P.L. 93-112):

✳ Prevents discrimination against those with disabilities

✳ Applies to institutions that receive federal grant monies

The Education Act of 1974 (P.L. 93-280) established two laws:

✳ The Education of the Handicapped Act Amendments of 1974 first mentioned "appropriate education" for all children with disabilities

✳ The Family Education Rights and Privacy Act gave parents and students over eighteen the right to review records in the student's personal file

The Education of All Handicapped Children Act of 1975 (P.L. 94-142):

✳ Mandated a "free and appropriate" public education for all children with disabilities, ensured due process rights, and mandated Individual Education Plans (IEPs), and Least Restrictive Environments (LREs)

✳ Is the core of federal funding for special education

✳ Passed in 1975 and went into effect in October 1977 (This paved the way for the current IDEA laws; see below.)

The Education of the Handicapped Act Amendments of 1983 (PL 98-199):

✳ Established services to facilitate school to work transition through research and demonstration projects

✳ Established parent training and information centers

✳ Provided funding for demonstration projects and research in early intervention and early childhood special education

The Carl Perkins Vocational Education Act of 1984 (P.L. 98-524):

✳ Authorized federal funds to support vocational educational programs. (The goal of this legislation is to improve access to those who have been underserved in the past or those who have "greater-than-average educational needs," including students with disabilities.)

✳ Amended in 1990 and 1991 (P.L. 101-391 and P.L. 102-103) and was renamed the Carl D. Perkins Vocational and Applied Technology Education Act

✳ Includes not only individuals with disabilities, but also those who are economically and educationally disadvantaged, those with limited English proficiency, individuals who participate in programs to eliminate sex bias, and those in correctional institutions

Education of the Handicapped Act Amendments of 1986 (P.L. 99-457):

✳ Mandated services for preschoolers and established a program
to help states develop a system of early intervention services for
infants

**The Technology-Related Assistance Act for Individuals with
Disabilities (P.L. 100-407):**

✳ Amended in 1994 (P.L.103-218) and updated as the Assistive
Technology Act of 1998 (P.L. 105-394) (ATA)

✳ Provided funding to develop comprehensive statewide technology-related assistance programs

✳ Established the definition of "assistive technology" as "any item,
piece of equipment, or product system . . . that is used to
increase, maintain, or improve the functional capabilities of
individuals with disabilities"

The newest legislation:

✳ Requires states to support a public awareness program related
to the availability and benefits of assistive technology devices
and services

✳ Promotes interagency coordination to improve access to assistive technology, and provides technical assistance and training

✳ Provides organizational structures that promote access to assistive technology, and provides outreach support to community
organizations that provide assistive technology or assist individuals in using assistive technology

The Americans with Disabilities Act of 1990 (ADA) (P.L. 101-336):

✳ Prohibits discrimination on the basis of disability at school, at
work, and in public accommodations

✳ Is not limited to organizations that receive federal funds

✳ Applies to both public and private nonsectarian schools, from day care to graduate school

The Education of the Handicapped Amendments of 1990 (P.L. 101-476), renamed the Individuals with Disabilities Education Act (IDEA):

✳ Authorized and expanded discretionary programs, mandated transition services, defined assistive technology devices and services, and added autism and traumatic brain injury to the list of categories of children and youth eligible for special education and related services

The Individuals with Disabilities Education Act Amendments of 1992 (P.L. 102-119):

✳ Addressed the Infants and Toddlers with Disabilities Program

The Individuals with Disabilities Education Act Amendments of 1997(IDEA '97) (P.L. 105-17):

✳ The current law, which is described in more detail the next section

State laws may vary and may go beyond what is provided in the federal law.

How the Law Affects Your Education

Three pieces of legislation are important you: The Individuals with Disabilities Education Act (IDEA '97), Section 504 of the Rehabilitation Act of 1993, and the Americans with Disabilities

Act (ADA). The IDEA legislation was amended in 1997 and is often referred to as IDEA '97. Students still in high school are protected by all three pieces of legislation. Section 504 and the Americans of Disabilities Act cover those in college and university. If you are still in high school, start with the IDEA section. If you plan to go off to college or begin working, read the 504 and ADA sections as well. For a quick look at how the law affects education at the high school and college levels, see the chart at the end of the chapter.

IDEA '97—The Individuals with Disabilities Education Act Amendments of 1997

The Individuals with Disabilities Act (IDEA) requires public schools to provide services to eligible students with disabilities. Before you can receive special education services, IDEA requires that you have an evaluation. If you are currently receiving special education services, you are probably familiar with that process. An evaluation includes information from parents, medical professionals, and school staff, and may include specific tests. The results of an evaluation are used to determine if you need and are qualified for special education help in school.

Once you have been evaluated and found to need special services, you have the right to the following:

* A Free and Appropriate Education. The appropriate services that meet your state's standards will be provided without cost to you or your parents.

* Appropriate Evaluation. Trained evaluators will use a variety of tests and procedures to gather information about you and your disability. The evaluation tools must not be racially or culturally discriminatory. The evaluation is intended to provide information that is educationally useful.

✳ Individual Education Plan (IEP). The school must develop a written statement that includes your present level of performance, measurable goals, services and supplementary aids and services to be provided, the modifications the school will provide to help you meet those goals, an explanation of your classroom placement, any modifications to be made when you take statewide or districtwide assessment tests, the date services and modifications will begin, how often you will receive services, where you will receive services, how long you will receive services, transition services to be provided, the rights (if any) you will continue to receive once you reach age twenty-one (if you are still in public school), an indication of how your progress will be measured, and how and when your parents will be notified of your progress. The IEP Team must also consider whether you require assistive technology devices. (See more about this in chapters 10 and 11.)

✳ Least Restrictive Environment. This section of IDEA makes the assumption that students with disabilities should be in classes with their nondisabled peers and that you will not be placed in special classes, receive separate instruction, or be removed from the regular school setting *unless* you will not be able to succeed in a regular education setting even with the use of aides and services.

✳ Parent and Student Participation in Decision Making. Parents and students are part of the decision-making process. Students should help design the IEP, expressing preferences and interests. If transition services are to be discussed, students *must* be included in IEP meetings.

✳ Procedural Safeguards. This section provides your parents with the right to:

Be notified and to agree to evaluations and any changes in your instruction

Access to your education records

Hearings in the case of disagreements

Procedures for the resolution of disagreements

According to the Office of Special Education Programs (OSEP), if parents disagree with the proposed IEP, they can request a due process hearing and a review from the state educational agency, if applicable. They can also appeal the state agency's decision to state or federal court. In most cases, services under IDEA '97 discontinue once you have graduated from high school. If you attend private school, the IEP regulations are somewhat different and vary from state to state.

Section 504 of the Rehabilitation Act of 1973

Section 504 is a civil rights law that prohibits discrimination on the basis of disability in public and private programs and activities that receive federal funds. This protects both high school students and students attending colleges that receive federal funds. Since most colleges receive at least some federal support, most provide services under Section 504. The language most often identified with this law follows:

> No otherwise qualified individual with handicaps in the United States . . . shall, solely by reason of her or his handicap, be excluded from the participation in, be denied the benefits of, or be subjected to discrimination under any program or activity receiving Federal financial assistance.

The law is intended to prevent discrimination and to eliminate barriers. Institutions receiving federal assistance are required to provide reasonable modifications, accommodations, or auxiliary aids that help students have access to, participate in, and benefit from the full range of educational programs and activities offered to all students on campus.

Section 504 qualifications. All students covered by IDEA are also covered by Section 504, but students who do not qualify for IDEA may be eligible for Section 504. In order to qualify, an individual must have a "physical or mental impairment" (this includes specific learning disabilities and organic brain syndromes) that *substantially limits* one or more life activities. This requirement is very important. Many people have disabilities, but they do not necessarily limit their life activities. For the purposes of this law, life activities include caring for oneself, performing manual tasks, walking, seeing, hearing, speaking, breathing, *learning*, or *working*. It is obvious that this law helps protect those with physical disabilities, but for you, it is important to note that learning and working are also included as *life activities*.

To qualify, you must also have a record of your disability. Interestingly, the law also covers you if you are "regarded as having impairment." This provision most often covers those being discriminated against because they have been misdiagnosed as having a disability.

Schools are responsible for identifying those students who have disabilities if they are still in primary or secondary school. But, the law changes in regard to those who are in college. Colleges and universities are required to let students know about the availability of services, aids, and adjustments, and to provide the name of the person who coordinates the school's Section 504 services, but they have no obligation to identify students with disabilities. If you are a college student, once you have been accepted, you are responsible for notifying the school of your disability and for requesting the necessary accommodations you will require. You are also required to show documentation of your disability.

The college will provide equal access to courses, programs, activities, services, and facilities. They must also provide reasonable and appropriate accommodations, modifications, and/or auxiliary aids (assistive devices).

If you need auxiliary aids to participate, the college is oblig-ated to provide aids that meet your needs. This doesn't mean, however, that they are required to provide the most sophisticated device available. According to the law, the aid must provide the student with "equal opportunity to obtain the same result, bene-fit, or level of achievement." You may believe that you need a lap-top computer to take your class notes. The school may believe that providing you with a copy of class notes meets their obligation. The law stipulates that the college must provide auxiliary aids unless they would cause "undue burden." Read more about assis-tive devices in chapter 15.

At the college level, students may receive accommodations to assist them in their coursework, but with those accommo-dations, they must be qualified to meet all of the program's re-quirements.

Colleges are not required to provide course waivers or changes in graduation requirements. You will need to discuss these issues with your school's Section 504 coordinator.

Unless authorized by you, the college must keep your disability information confidential.

Section 504 procedural safeguards. Complaints should be filed with the school's 504 compliance officer or the regional office of the Office for Civil Rights. Students and parents may also initi-ate a court action. It is not necessary to file a complaint with a federal agency before going to court. For more information, con-tact:

Disability Rights Section
Civil Rights Division
U.S. Department of Justice
P. O. Box 66738
Washington, DC 20035-6738

The Americans with Disabilities Act of 1990 (ADA)

The Americans with Disabilities Act (ADA) further prohibits discrimination on the basis of a disability. Title II of the ADA covers activities of state and local governments, including public education. Although it has no specific provisions regarding specific educational programs, the ADA also requires that schools make reasonable accommodations for handicapped individuals. ADA applies to both public and private nonsectarian schools, from day care to graduate school.

ADA qualifications.   The ADA language is similar to Section 504, but includes institutions that do not receive federal funding.

ADA procedural safeguards.   Complaints of Title II violations may be filed with the Department of Justice. In some situations, cases may be referred to a mediation program sponsored by the Justice Department.

A list of fundamental differences between services required at the high school and the college level is included in the chart on the following page.

Resources

ADA Information Line
    (800) 514-0301
    http://www.usdoj.gov/crt/
    ada/adahom1.htm.

EDLAW, LLC, and The EDLAW Center
    http://www.edlaw.net/

Educational Law Materials from Cornell University
    http://www.law.cornell.edu/
    topics/education.html

Americans with Disabilities Act Document Center
    http://janweb.icdi.wvu.edu/
    kinder/

The National Information Center for Children and Youth
with Disabilities
    http://www.nichcy.org

A Guide to Disability Rights Laws, U.S. Department of Justice.
    http://www.usdoj.gov/crt/ada/cguide.htm

Figure 12.1

High School Responsibilities	College Responsibilities
Identify students with learning disabilities	At the college level you must self-identify. You must let them know you have a learning disability and what services you need.
Education is a right and must be provided to all students.	Students must be qualified and meet admission criteria of the college.
Provide free testing and evaluations	Students must provide documentation and pay for evaluations if they are necessary
Schools develop individualized education programs, IEPs, to meet a students educational needs	The student must identify needs and request services. (A Disabilities Services Coordinator may work closely with the student to help arrange for accommodations and advocate for the student, but the student is required to contact the coordinator. At some schools the student must work directly with the professor.) Schools are not required to provide aides, services, or devices for personal use or study.
Programs may be altered	Schools are not required to alter requirements for admission or graduation. Schools must provide reasonable accommodations.
Required to keep you in school	Not required to keep you as a student. You have the right to fail.

Reviewing Postsecondary Education Options

Exploring Educational Options

If you have decided that you would like to continue your formal education after graduation from high school, this chapter is for you. As you begin the exploration process, it is important to consider whether you want to attend a four-year college, a junior college or community college, or a trade or vocational school. Maybe you would like to take a postgraduate year at a school that may provide you with the skills you may need for success at the college level.

As a student with a learning disability, you have many more options available to you than you might have had twenty years ago. According to the American Council on Education's HEATH Resource Center, twenty years ago, only thirty-five colleges and universities served students with learning disabilities. Federal legislation has changed that. Today, colleges and universities receiving federal funds provide accommodations that can help you compete on a level playing field with those who do not have disabilities. The most recent *Peterson's Guide of Colleges with Programs for Students with Learning Disabilities or ADHD* lists 750 colleges offering services.

Students who decide to continue with education after high school have more options than ever. Each choice has different admission criteria and a different set of goals. See the box for a quick view of some of your choices, and read on for more information.

Four-Year Degree Programs

Public or private four-year colleges and universities offer a wide variety of programs in a wide variety of settings. They can range from quite easy to get into with open enrollment policies up to very selective schools accepting only a small percentage of students who apply. These schools offer degree programs and many are residential. College guides in print or on line can give you specific information

OPTIONS AFTER HIGH SCHOOL

Four-Year Colleges and Universities
Private and State

The majority of colleges have four-year programs and offer degree programs. They range in size from very small private schools to city-sized urban institutions. These schools offer a range of programs. They also offer a range of services and accommodations for students with learning disabilities.

Community Colleges/Junior Colleges

Close to home and inexpensive, community colleges offer programs for students who would like to go directly into the workforce after two years and for students who would like to transfer and complete their final two years in a four-year school. Most have large numbers of learning disabled students enrolled and offer support services specifically designed for LD students.

Vocational Schools

For the student who wants a hands-on education and is job oriented, vocational schools provide specific training for specific jobs. If you know what you want to do, are not interested in exploring options, and are ready to prepare for a job, a vocational school may be right for you.

Postgraduate Schools/Nondegree Programs

Many schools now offer one- to two-year programs designed for students who are not quite ready for college. Some offer specialized summer programs. These programs are for students who need a little more time to mature, time to work on learning skills, or a chance to improve their academic record in order to qualify for a more competitive college.

Nondegree/Life Management Programs

Some programs are designed for students with more significant learning disabilities and may include social and life-skills training. Some are on college campuses and provide access to college facilities and experiences.

about these schools. Your search criteria might include location, size, program, extracurriculars, admissions criteria, housing, and so forth. Guides can help you narrow your search. Although schools receiving federal funds must offer at least minimal support services for students with learning disabilities, many four-year institutions offer more than that. Many schools today offer coordinated services or full comprehensive programs designed specifically for students with learning disabilities. Some four-year schools offer cooperative programs that allow students to work while they learn. If you know what kind of work you would like to do once you have finished college, this can be an excellent choice. Students are paid to work as they study and have personal introductions to the corporate world. Some programs allow you to attend classes for a semester and then work for a semester. Others provide for part-time work alongside of part-time study. If you enjoy hands-on learning, this may be for you.

Community College

According to recent statistics gathered by the American College on Education, more than half of the high school graduates with learning disabilities choose to enroll in community colleges. Why? Many high school students with learning disabilities aren't adequately prepared to enter a four-year college and university. They might have poor scores and low GPAs and not feel confident about getting into four-year programs or about doing the college-level work once they get there. Many community colleges have open enrollment policies, requiring only a high school diploma (sometimes even a GED is acceptable) for admission. Community colleges can accept students who need additional support because they offer remediation and support services designed to help students with learning disabilities succeed. This is often an excellent choice for students who need additional time to beef up their skills, explore career options, or to decide if entering a four-year college is a goal.

Not all students attending community college are there because they are not prepared for the challenges of a four-year college, however. Some students want to be close to home and others want to save money. Many students use a community college as a stepping-stone and transfer to four-year colleges once they have improved their scores and their grades. Some community colleges have transfer relationships with four-year schools and students are able to transfer all of their credits.

Not all students who attend community college have poor academic records, however. Many choose to attend a community college because it is more affordable. Students can save significant amounts of money by doing their first two years at a community college and then transferring to complete their degrees at a four-year insitution.

I want to work with kids with disabilities. I knew I wanted to do that all through high school. After high school, I found a course that would let me continue my education. Right now, I just finished the noncredit Early Childhood Training Program at Quinsigamond Community College. During the semester break, I am going to take the college placement tests then start my next course. I hope to work in a day care center and go to school at the same time. What would I say to someone thinking of college? I'd say, try it!

—A community college student

Community colleges are often very close to home. For some, this means a significant savings because they do not have to pay for on-campus housing. Others make the decision because they would like to have the support of family while they try out the college setting.

Some students opt to take part-time jobs and take community college classes in the evening. This provides an introduction to col-

lege level work and helps an unsure student know whether he or she is ready for college.

Many students just don't want to go to school for four more years. They are eager to enter the workforce and understand that specific, and often inexpensive, training is available at the community level. Some community colleges have relationships with businesses and corporations and students can take part in work/study programs. These two-year cooperative programs may offer associate's degrees or specific job certifications along with on-the-job training.

Vocational-Technical and Trade Schools

Some students know exactly what kind of job they want and they are eager to get the training necessary to secure that type of job.

Specialized vocational and trade schools are designed to give students the training they need to enter the workforce. Maybe you would like to work as a truck driver, or a carpenter, or a dental hygienist. Maybe you are interested in being a court reporter, a travel agent, an accountant, or a cook. There are many jobs out there that do not require college degrees. Your state's department of education can lead you to a vocational school that will meet your needs. You might also check out the resources at the end of this chapter.

Most vocational schools have open enrollment policies, though some require a high school diploma or GED.

College Prep Programs

Many private schools across the country offer a fifth year for high school students who need an opportunity to boost skills and grades. These prep schools can provide a transition experience from life at home with parents to a more independent college campus setting. Students generally live in dorms, have meals in dining halls, and have opportunities to participate in extraccurricular programs. Prep school students are more supervised than college students.

Some prep schools are designed specifically for students with learning disabilities and focus efforts on strengthening skills and providing learning strategies. Students who choose this route are generally those who are eager to become more competitive in their college searches. Those who attend the specialized programs haven't yet received the specialized skills training that can help them be more successful students.

Many prep schools have entrance requirements similar to colleges. Some require test scores and written essays. They may require a personal interview. This process can help students prepare for the more rigorous college application process.

Summer Prep Programs

Colleges across the county now offer summer progams to help students prepare for their first year in college. Some schools offer programs on their own campuses for incoming freshmen. In fact, at some schools participation in the summer program is mandatory for students accepted into a learning disabilities program. There are also colleges that run specialized precollege programs open to students regardless of where they will be going to school in the fall. These programs usually help students develop or improve the skills they will need and may help students with a variety of offerings that might include using college texts, taking notes, improving vocabulary, technology training, improving memory, strengthening writing skills, reading comprehension, and so on. Programs may be day programs or residential programs and run from two weeks to eight weeks. Costs vary according to the length of the program and whether or not students stay on campus. The HEATH Resource Center can provide a list of programs across the country. See the Resources list at the end of this chapter.

Nondegree Programs

Some students with significant learning disabilities choose nondegree programs that help provide job training and life-skills training. Some of these programs are independent commuter schools and others are located on college campuses and provide on-campus interaction and housing options. They offer comprehensive support and job training and may offer some college credit for work completed. These programs help students not only with academics and jobs but with social skills as well.

Making Choices

With those options in mind, the HEATH Resource Center and the Association of Higher Education and Disability (AHEAD) suggest asking yourself three questions before you narrow your search.

> Students here have a social group to be with.... Every weekend there is a movie night in one of the dorms. There is always some type of structured social program on weekend.
>
> —David Leslie,
> director,
> The Threshold Program
> Lesley University

1. How Prepared Are You?

If you have taken most of the steps recommended in the chapter on transition planning, you are probably ready for college. Can you manage your own money? Can you organize your time? Can you set priorities? Can you be academically successful with appropriate accommodations? If not, you may not be ready for a four-year program. You may want to consider a postgraduate program or a community college.

Are you self-motivated? If you choose to go away to school, you will be in charge. No one is going to be checking your homework, or monitoring whether or not you go to class, or seeing that you eat properly or get enough sleep. If you go away from home for school, you will be supervising your education and your life. Some students are more than ready for that challenge. Others need a little more time.

Have you considered the differences in the workload? Though you may be very successful in high school (maybe even without accommodations), college-level work will present additional challenges. Students who have received services in high school often want to try to "do it on my own" in college. Special services directors caution against trying that, saying there are critical differences between work at the college level and high school work. Figure 13.1 shows just a sampling of major academic differences.

As the chart on the following page indicates, much of what you do at the college level is self-directed. You will be spending half as much time in the classroom, but at least twice as much time on homework. How you spend your time outside of class will have a critical impact on your level of success.

Professors won't know how much time you spend on your work outside of class until they see your test performance. If you don't do well, they aren't going to call your Mom or Dad. In fact, your Mom and Dad won't even see your grades unless you show them.

> When I looked at the school, I didn't ask about the amount of work. I was more concerned about being able to get my car on campus.
>
> I asked when I got here and I was told it was about thirty hours a week! Last night I was up late and woke up early this morning to work.
>
> —Eric,
> a college freshman

The responsibility for success is yours. This is your time to do things because *you want* to do them. Ask yourself, "Do I really want to go to college?" and "Am I ready to work harder than I ever have before?" If *you* want to go to college, *you* are ready to work, and *you* want to do well, you have one of the basic ingredients for success: *motivation*.

2. Where Do You Want to Go to School?

Are you eager to leave home? Do you want to get a fresh start in a new environment? Or would you rather be close to your family and your family support system? Would you like to eat your meals at home and study in the comfort of your own room? Do you want to go to a large school where there may be more opportunities for academic choices but not as much support? Would you rather go to a smaller school? Do you want to be in the city, the suburbs, or in a rural area? The answers

Figure 13.1

Differences	High School	College
Work Hours	About 6 hours a day. 30 hours a week. Homework/Study time ranges from 1 to 3 hours a night or between 5 and 15 hours a week. Research Papers/Writing Assignments—maybe 1–2 (3 to 5 pages each) a semester.	12–16 hours in class. Minimum of 2 hours of study for every hour in class, or 30 hours a week. If it takes you longer to read, you will need even more time. Many lengthy research projects requiring weeks of preparation.
Grades	Many opportunities for graded assignments, making it relatively easy to make up for one poor test. Extra credit and homework assignments may bring your grades up. You can pass with a D. Your parents will monitor your grades.	Maybe only a mid-term, a final, and a paper will be graded. One bad grade can put you in jeopardy. No extra credit and generally no grades for homework. You may need a C average to graduate, and you may not be able to take the next level of required course work without a C. Your parents won't see your grades.

(Continued on next page)

Figure 13.1 (Continued)

Differences	High School	College
Class Size	Usually no more than 30–35.	Between 25 and 300.
Teachers/ Professors	Teachers have opportunities for direct contact with students each day. Teachers keep an eye on your homework and check your notebook. They remind you of deadlines and expect you to learn what is taught.	Students must schedule time to meet with professors and may only be able to meet with teaching assistant. Professors seldom check to see if you are doing your work. They expect you to work and to think on your own.

to these kinds of questions can help you decide if you want to go away to school or start out at a community college close to home.

What are your financial limitations? How much money is available for your college education? Can you and your family afford four years of college tuition, room and board, and expenses? Could your money go a little farther if you spent the first two years at a less expensive community college and then transferred for your last two years? Are your state schools less expensive than private schools? What are your opportunities for financial aid?

3. What Do You Want to Study?

Are you in a hurry to get into the job market? Are there specific skills that you can learn at a school close to home that will prepare you for that career in a year or two? Do you want to take time to explore more than one option and take a broader range of courses? Is there a particular program you are interested in that isn't offered everywhere or is there a particular job you are interested in that requires intensive study in a specialized program? What are your goals?

What are the entrance requirements for the schools you are interested in? Which schools have entering freshmen scores and statistics that match yours? (Not all schools require SAT test results. Some have open admissions and admit anyone over eighteen with a high school diploma.)

After reviewing the questions above, you may decide you don't want to go to college or that you don't want to go to college right now. You have alternatives. See more about alternatives, including military service, in the next chapter.

Search Tools

After answering questions about yourself, you can use college guides and Internet resources to help you explore your options. Several companies now publish college guides written especially for those with learning disabilities. These provide basic information about the schools as well as information about the school's disability services. Remember, however, information changes often. Before making any decisions, be sure to call the school to confirm information and the names of contact people.

College Web sites can allow you to take a virtual tour. Today you can visit the campus from the comfort of your home or your library. You can watch videos, hear interviews, exchange e-mail, and in some cases apply to the school directly on line. At the beginning of the search process, students with learning disabilities should look at colleges in the same way all students look at colleges. Does the school offer a program I am interested in? Is it the right size for me? Is it in an environment I think I will enjoy? Does it offer extracurricular activities I am interested in? Can I play a sport there? There are many resources to help you through this initial phase. A list of exploration resources is available at the end of this chapter.

Evaluating Programs

Once you have used the questions and resources to explore colleges, create a list of schools (ten to fifteen) that are of special interest to you. Once you have your list (based on the same criteria any student would use for selecting a college), you are ready to consider your special needs and the special services provided at the schools you are considering.

All students have strengths and weaknesses and need to appraise them before going to college. Students with learning disabilities have a more significant challenge. In order for you to evaluate a college on the basis of its services, you must understand your needs. Look at your high school experience to determine your level of need.

1. Are you receiving special education services? Did you need help daily, weekly, or for special projects? What type of help do you receive?
2. What subject areas or types of assignments are the most difficult for you?
3. What kinds of tests are difficult—essay, written exams, oral exams, etc.?
4. Do you have organizational problems? Problems with written work? Problems with keeping track of assignments?
5. Do you have problems with reading speed or reading comprehension?
6. Do you have problems with math or with foreign languages?
7. Do you have spatial problems?

8. How are your social skills?
9. Have you taken college preparatory courses in high school? How successful were you in those courses?
10. Have you learned strategies to help you compensate for your areas of weakness?

If the answers to these questions help you recognize areas of need, you are in a better position to evaluate the learning disabilities services a college has to offer. If you needed help on a regular basis in high school, it is likely you will need regular services in college. If you struggle with writing, you will want to find a school that has strong support services in that area. If your reading comprehension skills are weak, you will need strong supports in that area.

If, on the other hand, you sought out your special education teacher only when you needed to review for a test or when you needed some help organizing a term paper, schools with basic services may work for you.

Not all high school graduates are ready for college. Some need to boost their skills with special programs, some benefit from a post-graduate year at a college prep school, and some can benefit from sampling college by taking a course or two at a local community college. Some colleges also offer summer programs designed to help students with learning disabilities prepare for the work that is in store. Some students just aren't interested in college and are eager to prepare for a specific job. Your goals will help you make your choices.

It is up to you to decide the level of services you will need and to find the college or vocational school that provides what you want. Once you have evaluated your skills, you will be in a better position to evaluate the services schools have to offer. All schools receiving federal funds must offer services for students with learning disabilities. Some provide very basic services, some offer more specialized services, and some offer structured programs specifically designed to support the student with learning disabilities. Once you decide the level of services you think you will need, you can begin looking more closely at the colleges on your list. The director of disability services at each school can send you introductory information about the school's services.

Making the Match

If you needed little help in high school, a school offering basic services may be adequate. Schools offering basic services meet the federal guidelines mandating reasonable accommodations. The staff may not be trained to work with learning disabled students, but they are willing to provide basic accommodations to students who have documented learning disabilities. Smaller schools with lower student-to-teacher ratios can usually provide more individualized attention and that is something you will want to keep in mind if you decide basic services are sufficient.

If you needed more than occasional services in high school, you will most likely need more than basic services. Many schools offer coordinated services administered by at least one learning disabilities specialist. At some schools, this specialist is involved in the admission process and may be able to provide some expertise in evaluating the application of an LD student. In addition to arranging for classroom and testing modifications, these schools may offer specific skills courses, specialized summer programs, and/or remedial programs. These schools may require placement tests after admission to help you find the right academic course level.

As more and more students with learning disabilities are going to college, more colleges are offering comprehensive programs. These schools may offer specialized courses in reading, speaking, study skills and learning strategies, writing, or time management. They may provide tutoring. Students who received regular help while they were in high school, students who did not take college preparatory courses, and students who needed tutoring or who had course requirements modified may want to consider schools with comprehensive programs. At these schools, the faculty is experienced in teaching students with learning disabilities and with providing accommodations to help them succeed. If you believe you could benefit from an increased level of support, this type of program is probably best for you. At some of these schools, you apply directly to the program.

Once you have evaluated the programs of the schools already on your list, you will have narrowed your search sufficiently to begin fine-tuning. Your list should now include five to ten schools you think offer what you are looking for. At this point, you will want to visit the schools on your list and talk to the people responsible for providing services. Call the admission offices of the schools on your list and make appointments for tours and interviews.

How Does It Feel?

Most students know when they walk on a campus if the school feels right for them. They just have a sense that it is the right fit. That is probably the most important factor in deciding whether a college will make your final application list. If you aren't comfortable there, no matter what program they offer, what supports they provide, or what extracurricular activities are available, you probably won't be successful there.

Talk to Students

Talk to students while you are on campus. Ask them what they like best about the school and what they are unhappy about. Ask about social activities. (Also check the school's bulletin boards and the school newspaper for listings of social events.) Ask about the food.

If at all possible, talk to students who are receiving accommodations. The director of disability services should be able to arrange that for you. Are their accommodations working for them? Are the professors receptive to requests for accommodations? Is it easy to meet with the program director to discuss accommodations and/or problems?

Meet with the Disability Services Coordinator

When you meet with the program director, prepare a list of questions to ask. The list we provide here can help you get started, but you should develop your own list with questions that are specific to your disability and to your needs. You should ask the questions. Of course, your parents will want to be involved in the conversation, but this is one of the times you can practice advocating for yourself. *You* are going to go to the school, *you* are going to need the services, *you* are going to work with this person; you need to be involved. You also need to understand the differences between your high school's legal obligations to provide service and the college's legal level of obligation. If you don't already know this, read chapter 12 and look at the chart on high school and college responsibilities.

You should also be prepared to answer questions, especially about your disability. If you are a good self-advocate, you will be able to explain your learning disability and the types of accommodations you believe you will need.

Do you feel comfortable with the services coordinator? This is the person you will need to go to in order to arrange for accommodations, for support when you need help, and for guidance. You want to feel you can talk to this person and that this person understands your needs.

Ask for a tour of the school's academic resource center. If the resource center is for all students, are people there who can help students with learning disabilities? If the school has a support center

QUESTIONS FOR THE LEARNING DISABILITY
SERVICES COORDINATOR

1. Is tutoring available? Are tutors trained to work with students with learning disabilities?
2. What accommodations are available for students like me? Are reading materials available on tape? Can I get extended time for tests or assignments? Can I use my calculator in math classes? Can the format of tests be altered to meet my needs? Are note takers or scribes available? Are assistive technologies available? Is training available? How do I arrange to receive accommodations? How do I access special equipment?
3. Does the school have someone available who is trained and understands the needs of college students with learning disabilities?
4. Where are support programs offered?
5. Is there a learning center specifically for students with learning disabilities? If not, is there anyone trained in learning disabilities in the college support centers—the writing center, the computer labs, the math lab, etc.?
6. Is there someone who can help me with course selection?
7. Is early registration for courses an option?
8. Is academic and/or career counseling available?
9. Are mentors available?
10. What other services are provided?
11. What, exactly, do I need to do to qualify for services? What documentation is required?
12. Do I need to apply to a specialized program to receive services?
13. What documentation will I need to receive services?
14. Are SATs or ACTs required? Are non-standard scores accepted?
15. What percentage of students graduate? Ask about specifically about LD students as well. Is there is a specialized program for LD students? These figures should be available.

Adapted from the "How to Choose a College" HEATH Resource Center specifically for students with learning disabilities, be sure to visit. Ask what types of supports they provide and what technologies are available there that might benefit you.

Check Out the Library

College-level work requires more research and writing than high school. Although students with learning disabilities can use student support services to help them in these areas, they often undervalue the importance of a good library with accessible holdings. A good library will be close by, will have comfortable and adequate space for the students, will have areas designated for group study and for individual, quiet study, will be open when you need to use it, and will have adequate resources to answer your research questions. Check the electronic card catalog to see if the library has resources specific to your planned major. Do they have periodicals related to your field of study? Does the library offer electronic tools for locating and retrieving magazine and journal articles? Can you get full text of the articles? Does the library belong to an interlibrary loan program? Can you access the library's card catalog from your dorm room? Talk to some of the people there. Do they seem friendly and helpful? Do they offer electronic support, such an answers to e-mail questions? You can expect to spend time in the library once you are a student at that school. Be sure you feel comfortable there.

Review Entrance and Graduation Requirements

In order to be successful at a particular college, you must get in. You must also graduate. Unfortunately, it is much easier to get into school than to graduate. Some colleges have admissions requirements that you may not have met. If the college you are interested in has a two-year high school foreign language requirement, and you only took one year, you may not qualify for admission. Ask if waivers of admission requirements are ever granted and under what circumstances. If the graduation requirement for the program you are interested in requires advanced mathematics courses and you were unsuccessful in math in high school, ask if graduation requirements are ever waived and under what circumstances. You don't want to select a college that has requirements you cannot possibly meet. Some schools will allow course substitutions. Ask under what circumstances and how often substitutions are allowed.

Housing Options

For students with learning disabilities, the housing options available on or off campus may play an important role in the likelihood of success or failure. Some colleges and universities offer housing for all freshmen students. Students may be housed in on-campus dormitories in single, double, triple, or quad rooms.

> Dorm life is a disorganized, disorienting experience. It may not be a personal failure not to live in a dorm ... sometimes students are better off in an apartment with a few people.... Sometimes they thrive on dormitory life.
> —Eileen Berger, director, Office of Disability Services Salem State College

At some schools, freshmen students are required to live on campus. Not all schools guarantee housing for freshmen students. Students are sometimes required to live in off-campus apartments. You need to consider your specific needs when thinking about housing. Some students can't concentrate or study in a dormitory and would be better served in a small apartment. Other students need the interaction of other students and would feel isolated off campus.

Although supervision is minimal in most dormitory settings, some students need at least some level of supervision. At some schools, more than half the students live off campus. Because most of the students are commuters and don't live on campus, these schools often don't have the same weekend social offerings or extracurricular activities. Be sure to ask about housing options when you visit and choose schools that provide the right solutions to your housing needs.

Applications

Application to college has never been easier. Students in the past had to type a different application form for each school without the technology taken for granted today. There was no cut and paste option, no spell check, and no grammar check.

Today, many colleges accept common applications and many even accept on-line applications. The information you gather while you are visiting schools will include application information, including deadlines. In general, application packages require the application, the high school transcript, and an essay or personal statement. Many students with learning disabilities decide to disclose their disability by writing about its impact on their lives in the college essay. Those who can write about their disabilities in a positive way, explaining how they have overcome or learned to cope with their disabilities, can help admission committees understand discrepancies between intellectual ability and grades or test scores. Of course, you may choose to write about something else. That's fine, too. Remember that this is your opportunity to let the schools learn about you. Allow yourself plenty of time to develop your essay, be sure someone else reads it (a guidance counselor or special education teacher, for example), be sure you spell check it and be sure to have another human being spell check it as well. Don't submit it until you feel it is the best essay you can write.

SATs/ACTs

The ACT and the SAT are standardized tests required for admission by some colleges and universities. The SAT is a three-hour exam that measures two sets of skills—verbal and mathematical reasoning. The verbal

> I take longer to do things. . . . I couldn't finish the SATs. After I was diagnosed, I took the SATs untimed.
>
> —Eric, a college freshman

section tests your ability to understand and analyze what you read, recognize relationships between parts of a sentence, and establish relationships between pairs of words. The math section tests your ability to solve problems involving arithmetic, algebra, and geometry.

The second part of the SAT or the SAT II covers specific subject areas. These tests are normally one hour in length. Your high school guidance counselor will have information on these tests.

The ACT is a national college admissions exam that consists of tests in English, reading, mathematics, and scientific reasoning. The test is made up of 215 multiple-choice questions.

Some students with documented learning disabilities may qualify for reasonable accommodations on the test, or nonstandardized test administration. This "nonstandardized" format may include additional time or large print booklets and answer sheets. Audiocassette versions of the test and test readers or answer writers may also be available. Students who need to take medications may be given permission to take them during the testing period. Since many students with learning disabilities take longer to read and/or to process what they have read, the extended time option is the most often requested accommodation. Your high school guidance counselor can help you determine if you will need to take a nonstandard version of the test.

Documentation

In order to qualify for accommodations at the college level, you will need to submit documentation, or proof, that you actually have a learning disability that *substantially* limits your ability to learn. College requirements for documentation may vary slightly, but the guidelines in the box provide a general overview of what will probably be expected.

Evaluators must be qualified and their credentials must be included along with the evaluation. Because documentation must be current (no more than two to three years old, depending on the college), it is

DOCUMENTATION BASICS

- A qualified professional must conduct the evaluation.
- Testing must be current.
- Documentation must include:
  diagnostic interview
  assessment
  a specific diagnosis
  test scores
  accommodations

An interpretive summary should also be included.

wise to be reevaluated just before high school graduation. This reevaluation can be a part of your transition plan (see chapter 11).

The documentation must reflect your current level of disability. Although your high school IEP can be part of the documentation, it alone is insufficient. A thorough diagnostic interview will include reports, interviews, test scores, and transcripts that are relevant to the particular disability and the necessary accommodations.

The assessment will include an evaluation of aptitude or cognitive ability, academic achievement, and information processing, and will rely on the results of more than one test. Actual test scores must be provided.

The diagnosis of a learning disability must be specific and should include the words "disorder" or "disability," not general terms such as "learning styles" or "learning differences." Although many students resent the terms "disorder" and "disability," if they are to receive accommodations at college, their documentation *must* include those terms. The accommodations recommended must be accommodations that are needed now, not those that the student may or may not have received in the past, and the report must explain why accommodations are recommended. The evaluating professional will present his or her assessment in an interpretive summary of the information provided in the report.

An explanation of testing and a review of some of the most frequently used tests are included in chapter 9. The director of disability services at the college you are interested in can give you specific information about the school's documentation requirements.

Disclosure

Some students disclose their learning disability on their essay. For

> It shouldn't hurt to let the school know (about a learning disability), because if it is a problem for them, it's not a place where you want to go to school.
>
> —Scott,
> a college freshman

> Students need to understand that an institution of higher education cannot discriminate against them if they identify themselves as having a learning disability during the application process.... Too often they are reluctant to identify. I strongly encourage them to.... They can bring so much to an institution. Until they identify, their weaknesses can be used against them.
>
> —Chip Kennedy,
> disability services
> coordinator,
> Babson College

some, nonstandard SAT scores notify the college of a disability. You need to decide whether or not to disclose your learning disability. Professionals we spoke to saw no advantage in hiding a learning disability, but you are not required to disclose it. Colleges and universities cannot discriminate on the basis of a disability. If you choose not to disclose your disability when you apply, you must inform the disabilities services office of your need and provide your documentation once you have been accepted.

Students with learning disabilities have more opportunities now than ever before. Between 1988 and 1998, *learning disabled* was the fastest growing *disability category* reported by college freshmen, jumping from 15.3 to 41 percent! Today, there are close to 200,000 students with learning disabilities in postsecondary educational settings. No matter what you choose to study after high school, there are opportunities for you.

Maybe, however, you just don't want to study anymore. Or maybe you want to take a break. There are many opportunities open to you. Read the next chapter.

Resources

Internet Resources for Postsecondary Education

Students don't have to wait for those college informational packets anymore. They don't have to rely solely on their school guidance counselors or college information nights. Today, students can begin college searches at home or at the library by visiting Internet sites that provide information on colleges, applications, testing, student evaluations, and so forth. Many of these sites provide direct links to college Web pages and some of them provide virtual tours. These sites are free, but most require you to register to use all of their services. Let the search begin.

College Board

www.collegeboard.com

College Board Online offers information on the SATs, financial aid, college searches, and you can try your luck answering the SAT question of the day.

College Link

www.collegelink.com

Includes a college search, financial aid, scholarship, and an online application feature. This site also has information on scholarships and loans.

Embark

www.embark.com

Resources for college searches and test preparation and online application options.

HEATH Resource Center

http://www.heath-resource-center.org

The American Council on Education's HEATH Resource Center is filled with information for students with disabilities, including learning disabilities. They offer an excellent pamphlet, "How to Choose a College: Guide for the Student with a Disability." Visit their Web site for more information.

Princeton Review

www.review.com

Provides college information, test prep information, career interest surveys, and student discussion groups. Links to APPLY! where you can download college applications.

RWM Vocational School Database
http://www.rwm.org/rwm/states.html
A list of vocational schools provided by state departments of education.

U.S. News Online
www.usnews.com
At the U.S. News Web site, go to the education link and from there to colleges. This site offers traditional college search information as well as personality quizzes, organizers, scholarship searches, grade calculators, admission tips, and more.

Print Resources

Doliber, Roslyn. *College and Career Success for Students with Learning Disabilities.* Chicago: VGM Career Horisons, 1996.

Dravets, Marybeth, and Imy F. Wax. *The K&W Guide to College for Students with Learning Disabilities.* 5th ed. New York: Random House, 2001.

Mangrum, Charles T., and Stephen S. Strichart. *Colleges with Programs for Students with Learning Disabilities or Attention Deficit Disorders.* Princeton, N.J.: Peterson's, 2000.

Peterson's Guide to Vocational and Technical Schools West 2000. Princeton, N.J.: Peterson's Guides, 2000.

Peterson's Guide to Vocational and Technical Schools East. Princeton, N.J.: Peterson's, 1996. (This is currently out of print, but should be available at your local library.)

No More Teachers, No More Books

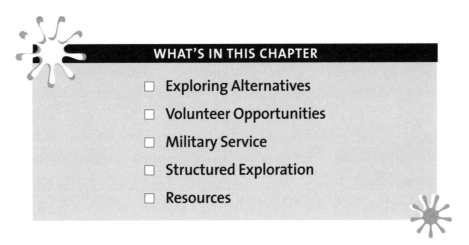

WHAT'S IN THIS CHAPTER

☐ Exploring Alternatives

☐ Volunteer Opportunities

☐ Military Service

☐ Structured Exploration

☐ Resources

Exploring Alternatives

Some students don't want to continue their education in the conventional way. They are eager to explore alternatives and to have life experiences that no longer put them in the traditional role of student. Some are demoralized by their time in school and have no interest in continuing what they consider a losing battle by spending more time in a classroom. Some students want to serve—their community, their country, or humankind. Some students have poor academic skills but creative strengths that have gone undervalued in a school setting. Others have been accepted to college, but have serious questions about what they hope to accomplish there. Any of these students may someday decide to continue their education, but they need to do something else first. Maybe you fall into one of these categories. Maybe your parents, your relatives, your friends think you should go to college, but you just know it isn't the right choice for you. Still, you don't want to sling hamburgers for the rest of your life. Don't despair. There are many opportunities out there that have nothing to do with schoolwork.

Of course, that doesn't mean you stop learning. You just learn in a new way. Some refer to this time as "taking time off," but that's not a great idea. No parent is eager to tell friends, "My son or daughter is 'taking time off.'" This causes the imagination to see a child lazing away day after day in an endless round of television shows or hanging out at the mall with friends. If you want to take time away from school, you will need a plan. Unless your plan includes a paid work experience, you will also need money. Some students choose to work for a few months after high school to earn enough to allow them to explore other options. There are settings that provide room and board in exchange for work and there are job opportunities in other countries that only require funds for transportation there. Some opportunities provide transportation as well. Depending on your family resources (and of course opinions about the plan), some parents choose to help their children take a year to explore options. Try calling this time between high school and college or high school or traditional work as a period of "international studies," "cultural exchange," or "humanitarian service." Your parents are probably much more likely to listen to you if put those tags on your goals.

There are more experiences available than could possibly be included in just a chapter of a book. What we offer here is a sampling to whet your appetite. We have included at the end of this chapter some of the resources we used to get us started, but there are many more out there. Once you start exploring, you will be amazed at the number of opportunities there are.

Colin Hall (who took time off before college to work and travel in Africa) and Ron Lieber gathered stories from more than thirty young people who made unusual choices after high school. Some took jobs in foreign country in order to learn more about another culture. Some did volunteer work in the United States or abroad. Several traveled, by foot, by train, or by bike. Their stories make interesting and inspirational reading. See their book in the Resources section below.

Volunteer Opportunities

The Corporation for National Service works with governor-appointed state commissions, nonprofits, faith-based groups, schools, and other organizations to provide opportunities for Americans to serve. One of the programs under their supervision is Americorps.

The Americorps motto is "Give Back for a Year. Serve Your Community. Change Your Life." There are hundreds of opportunities here for young people to serve, to learn, and to grow. So what is Americorps? Their Web page describes it as "the domestic Peace Corps" involving young people in more than 1,000 projects. Danielle Wood, in her book *The Uncollege Alternative*, calls it "a warm and fuzzy version of the military—an *un*-armed forces." Most Americorps members are selected by and serve with projects like Habitat for Humanity, the American Red Cross, the Boys' and Girls' Clubs, and other local and national organizations.

Included under the Americorps umbrella are Americorps/VISTA (Volunteers in Service to America) and Americorps/NCCC (the National Civilian Community Corps). VISTA volunteers serve economically challenged communities. Volunteers serve full-time and live in the communities they serve, helping to create programs that can continue after volunteer service is completed.

NCCC volunteers help in the areas of education, public safety, the environment, and other human needs. NCCC volunteers work for ten months in a full-time residential service program. As many as one-third of their volunteers come straight from high school. Volunteers might tutor or mentor children, help clean up the Chesapeake Bay, build a house, work on an archeological dig, build trains, or turn empty lots into gardens. Some positions allow young people to relocate and travel during their terms of service.

Interested in sports? NCCC volunteers have worked with Olympic officials and the Paralympics helping with construction projects, volunteer supervision, and crowd control. Want to help when disaster strikes? NCCC volunteers have helped fight forest fires and worked with the Red Cross helping tornado victims. Not only does this kind of experience give your résumé a boost, there are educational stipends attached to the programs. Volunteers receive training, a modest living allowance, health insurance, and an educational award to help pay for college or vocational training. For more information, see the Resources section at the end of this chapter.

Military Service

Want free training? Want money for college? Want to be better qualified for the job you are interested in? Want to get paid too?

Do you like structure? Do you thrive in challenging situations? Do you want to be active?

Military service might be for you. Any mention of military service calls to mind tanks during Desert Storm, peacekeeping forces in Somalia, or dangerous assignments in Afghanistan. Of course, that kind of work appeals to some young people. If so, combat services might just what you are looking for.

Most young people, however, don't realize that the military also needs carpenters and plumbers, office workers and computer technicians, brochure writers and public relations personnel. They need people who can do electrical maintenance and electrical equipment repair, operate machines, and deliver health care. In fact, if you can think of a job in civilian life, there is probably a corresponding job in the military.

All branches of the military take students just out of high school as enlisted personnel. Eighty-five percent of those in the Armed Forces are involved in enlisted careers. A sampling of positions available for enlisted personnel include:

Administrative Careers

Think you would like office work? People in these positions help with the paperwork involved in planning and managing military operations. They may type, maintain files, or work in specialized areas such as finance, accounting, legal, maintenance, or supply.

Combat

Want to maneuver against enemy forces or destroy enemy positions? Want to drive a tank or an amphibious assault vehicle? This job category is for those who are willing to be involved in difficult and dangerous missions. Combat specialists might be involved in offensive raids, demolitions, intelligence, or search and rescue missions, from aircraft, helicopters, ships, or submarines.

Construction Occupations

Enlisted men and women help build and repair military buildings, airfields, bridges, foundations, dams, and bunkers, and take care of the electricity and plumbing involved in military structures. You might operate a bulldozer or another piece of heavy construction equipment or work with engineers on a construction team.

Electrical and Electrical Equipment Repair

Want to repair computers? Would you rather work on weapons systems? Those involved in electrical repair often specialize in a particular type of equipment—avionics, computers, communications, or weapons systems. Enlisted personnel might also be involved with computer systems and software programs. They may repair spacecraft ground control equipment or specialize in repairing the equipment that tracks spacecraft locations.

Health Care

Interested in medicine? Enlistees interested in health care might work as part of a patient service team. As part of a team, you might provide emergency medical treatment, operate X-ray or ultrasound equipment, or maintain patient records.

Human Resources

You might work with recruiters providing information about military careers to other young people and their families. You might be involved in collecting and storing information about military careers, including training, job assignments, promotions, and health information.

Machine Operators and Production Careers

Want to work with or construct heavy equipment? This might be your area. The military needs welders to do metal repair or to form structural parts of ships, submarines, buildings, and so on. You might be responsible for repairing the survival equipment for airplanes.

Public Affairs and the Media

Like photography? Interested in video production? Enlisted personnel might take photographs, or film, record, and edit audio and video productions. Interested in broadcast journalism? You could work on news programming. Like to draw? You could find your career in producing graphic artwork or other visual displays.

Protective Service

Want to help in an emergency? You could be involved in responding to floods, earthquakes, hurricanes, or enemy attack. You could be involved in preventing crime or you could be a guard at a military correctional facility. You could also be a firefighter on the ground, in the air, or aboard ships.

Support Services

See yourself as a chef? You could be dishing it up on a ship, in a hospital, or in a dining hall.

Human Services

Interested in helping people work out their social problems? You could be part of a team that includes social workers, psychologists, medical offers, and chaplains. You can even be a religious specialist and help chaplains with services and religious education programs.

Transportation and Material Handling

You could specialize in moving people and cargo. You could be operating equipment on an airplane or driving a fuel or water tank truck; you could be piloting small boats, or you could be using a forklift to unload military supplies.

Vehicle and Machinery Mechanics

Like to tinker with engines? Don't mind getting your hands dirty? You could be an aircraft mechanic and repair or service helicopters or airplanes. You could work on self-propelled missile launchers, or you could cool your heels repairing air conditioning or refrigeration equipment. There is no end of equipment that needs repair in the military.

If you're not sure where you fit in, the Armed Services Vocational Aptitude Battery (ASVAB) may help you determine the best fit. The test measures your aptitude for success in different jobs. It consists of ten short individual tests covering word knowledge, paragraph comprehension, arithmetic reasoning, mathematics knowledge, general science, auto and shop information, mechanical comprehension, electronics information, numerical operations, and coding speed. You can use the results of the test in combination with the ASVAB Workbook. The book includes activities that help match interests, abilities, and personal preferences to more than 200 civilian and military careers. You can use the results with Military Careers, a career information resource, to determine your chances of qualifying for different military occupations. You can view a sample of the test at http://www.goarmy.com/util/asvab1.htm.

If you qualify, the military will pay you, train you in a specialty, house you, feed you, and help pay for your education once you have finished. Of course, you need to make a substantial commitment to them in return. Enlistment contracts call for up to eight years of service. Depending on the branch of the military and on the terms of the contract, two to six of those years are on active duty and the rest are spent in the reserves. And, of course, you must complete basic training, and I am sure you have seen at least one movie depicting that experience. This is how the Bureau of Labor Statistics describes it: "A 6–11-week introduction to military life with courses in military skills and protocol." They say, "Days and nights are carefully structured and include rigorous physical exercises designed to improve strength and endurance and build unit cohesion."

Once basic training is over, recruits receive formal training for a particular military specialty. Time for training ranges from ten to twenty weeks up to a year.

Recruits can sometimes receive college credit for training they receive on duty. For those who want to go to school during off-duty time, tuition assistance is available for correspondence courses or even degree programs at local colleges or universities.

No entry-level job gives as much vacation time as the military— 30 days of paid vacation a year—and, if you choose to make the military a career, you can retire after twenty years. That would make you about thirty-eight years old.

Each branch of the military has its own recruitment package and eligibility requirements. You can find out more about careers in the Army, Navy, Marines, Coast Guard, Air Force, and the Air and Army National Guard from your high school guidance counselor and you can get specific information at your local recruitment office.

Section 504 of the Rehabilitation Act does not cover uniformed personnel branches of the armed forces, so they are not required to provide accommodations. Students with diagnosed learning disabilities and attention deficits and those who might be taking medication will want to discuss that when being evaluated for military service. All medical conditions will be discussed as part of the qualification criteria. With specific goals in mind and with the opportunity to work within their areas of strength, students with learning disabilities can find opportunities in the military. Information about military careers is also available at the Military Career Guide online, http://www.militarycareers.com, and each branch of the military has its own Web page.

Structured Exploration

If you could wave a magic wand, what would you do? The Center for INTERIM Programs in Cambridge, Massachusetts, has been asking that question of young people for more than twenty years. Founded by Cornelius Bull in 1980, INTERIM provides a consulting/advisory/referral service for young people who want to explore alternatives to college. They call it "time on." INTERIM Programs provide information on opportunities in every region of the United States and in most other countries. Here, you can get multireferrals and take on several experiences over the course of a year or two. If you are not sure what kind of work you want to do, you have the opportunity to sample. Maybe you would like to try some active work that includes recreational activities. You might choose to spend a few months teaching young students to rock-climb, whitewater canoe, or backpack at an Outdoor Educational Training School in Virginia. Then, perhaps you could do a few months of conservation work in New Zealand. Maybe you would like to experience a totally different

> I don't believe anyone should go to college at 18.... If you are not ready to have an intellectual epiphany in college, you miss the whole point of the damn thing.
> —Cornelius Bull, Center for Interim Programs

> With the internships, I relaxed about school. The experience helped me mature and look at myself in a more positive way.... Taking time off is not a bad thing. It is more important to take the time to stop and think.... I do not think I would have a 3.2 GPA now if I had not taken time off.
> —Andrew Campbell, Delaware County Community College student

culture. You could spend time teaching English to young children in Katmandu. INTERIM provides referrals to almost 3,500 programs, so your chance of finding something that fits you is good.

Andrew Campbell helped raise animals as part of the Heifer Ranch Project, where he says the motto is "don't give a cup of milk, give a cow." He learned to take responsibility not only for the water buffalo he cared for, but also for himself. He ventured farther from home when he went to study whales in Hawaii, collecting information for the Island Marine Institute. He says the experiences helped him to mature, to be more independent, and to be more confident about his strengths. By the time he had finished with his INTERIM experiences, he was ready to go back to school.

INTERIM charges a fee ($1,900) for its counseling services and does not guarantee placements in specific programs. A few programs offer stipends, but for the most part these are unpaid positions. Some may provide room and board in exchange for labor, some charge a small fee for living expenses or a larger fee for tuition (usually for group programs with leaders and/or teachers). Students may take time between assignments to earn money to help pay for the experience.

Holly Bull, daughter of the program's founder, heads an affiliate office in Princeton, N.J., and Bull's sons, Neil and Sam, run an affiliated program for students west of the Mississippi. Their LEAPNow Program will also help organize two years of unlimited placements and help you find what they call the "juice" in your life.

Interested in animals? You could receive free housing while you work in a wildlife sanctuary in Maryland. Interested in art? You can get an introduction to the art and gallery world by working for an American artist at an artist's colony in the south of France. Interested in the environment? An outdoor ranch in New Mexico offers students an opportunity to work in an experimental, educational setting (a private elementary school in Albuquerque) working hands-on to explore ecology and the natural environment. For an additional fee, LEAPNow can arrange for students to take Internet courses allowing them to earn college credit during their work experience.

They have a database of more than 20,000 internships, apprenticeships, volunteer opportunities, study abroad programs, alternative educational experiences, and work exchanges in the United States and around the world. A few pay a stipend, some require additional fees, and some qualify for college credit.

Whether you are interested in art, the environment, social service, wildlife, the outdoors, or teaching, these referral agencies can help you explore alternatives at a cost far less than a year's college tuition.

Motivated students could find many of these opportunities without paying the referral fee, but Bull and his family take some of the risk out of searching for alternatives. They or one of their colleagues can vouch for the programs in their databases. More than 350 young people take part in INTERIM programs each year.

If you aren't sure what you are looking for, but you know you don't want to go to college right now, start your research with the resources listed below.

Resources

Americorps Volunteers
http://americorps.org

Center for Interim Programs
http://www.interimprograms.com

Hall, Colin, and Rob Lieber. *Taking Time Off: Inspiring Stories of Students Who Enjoyed Successful Breaks from College and How You Can Plan Your Own.* New York: Farrar, Straus & Giroux, 1996.

Lee, Linda. *Success without College.* New York: Doubleday, 2000.

Military Career Guide Online
http://www.militarycareers.com/

Naval Reserve
1-800-USA-USNR

United States Air Force
1-800-423-USAF
http://www.airforce.com

United States Army
1-800-USA-ARMY
http://usarmy.com/

United States Coast Guard
1-877-NOW-USCG
http://www.uscg.mil/

United States Marines
1-800-MARINES
http://www.marines.com

United States Navy
1-800-USA-NAVY
www.navyjobs.com

Wood, Danielle. *The Uncollege Alternative.* New York: HarperCollins, 2000.

Assistive Technology

WHAT'S IN THIS CHAPTER

☐ New Laws, New Technologies, New Success Stories

☐ Assistive Technologies

☐ Resources

New Laws, New Technologies, New Success Stories

Although many students with learning disabilities have learned to compensate with low-tech, or no-tech accommodations, innovative changes in technology have created new resources for those who need additional tools. Equipment only imagined in science fiction novels and movies when your parents were children is now available to help. Computers that not only provide print material but also speak to their "readers" are commonplace. Scanners allow individual pages and worksheets to be loaded into computers for reading or listening. Talking watches and voice-activated day planners provide help to those with poor planning skills.

253

Changes in the law have helped students use new technology. IEP teams are now required to discuss alternative technology as an option for helping students with learning disabilities. Colleges and universities are expected to accommodate students by providing alternative devices to help students there.

These changes have helped more and more students succeed in high school and have contributed to the increase in the numbers of learning-disabled students now attending and succeeding in college. See the chart in figure 15.1.

Both the Technology-Related Assistance for Individuals with Disabilities Act of 1998 and the Individuals with Disabilities Education Act of 1990 define assistive technology as "any item, piece of equipment, or product system, whether acquired commercially off-the-shelf, modified, or customized, that is used to increase, maintain or improve functional capabilities of individuals with disabilities." The

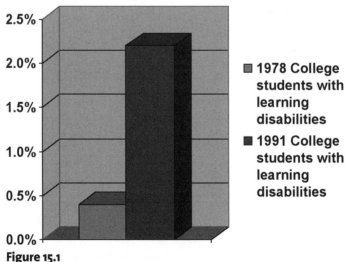

Figure 15.1
Percentage of College Students with Learning Disabilities
In 1978, 0.4 percent of college freshmen reported having a learning disability. In 1991 the numbers had increased more than five times to 2.2 percent.

legislation is also intended to assist schools, students, and parents in identifying and selecting the appropriate technology.

Assistive technologies can help you in two ways. They can help improve your skills or they can help compensate for your areas of weakness. In the elementary and middle school years, these technologies are most often used in an attempt to remediate or improve the learning disabled student's skills. At the high school level, new technologies may be used in the same way, but are often used to compensate for a student's disability as well. By the college level, assistive technology is most often used to improve a student's performance by compensating for an area of weakness.

All of us use tools to help us succeed. People have used highlighters to identify important pieces of information for years. Most students use a dictionary or a computer spell checker to assure correct spelling. Students with learning disabilities should view these new tools for success as simply that, "tools." Unfortunately, some students view these devices as "cheaters." That's ridiculous. If you have an identified learning disability and you qualify to use these new technologies, using them simply helps level the playing field. In fact, the law provides not unfair advantage, but just the opposite—equal opportunity.

Title II of the ADA states: "A public entity shall furnish appropriate auxiliary aids and services where necessary to afford an individual with a disability an *equal opportunity* to participate in, and enjoy the benefits of, a service, program, or activity conducted by a public entity."

Assistive technologies can be as simple as a special pencil grip to facilitate writing or as sophisticated as an optical character recognition (OCR) system that can scan and convert written text into computerized speech. There are hundreds of devices and programs designed to help students who have problems with organization, reading, listening, math, writing, and social skills.

The devices and programs listed here are intended to give an overview of what is available. This is in no way a comprehensive list of everything available today or what will be available by the time this book is published. It is intended to give you an idea of the variety of assistive technologies that can help with specific problems. Nor is the listing intended to be a recommendation. Each student is different, with different needs. What is helpful to one student is not necessarily the ideal device for another. Devices used to compensate in one area may also be used to strengthen another area as well. A multisensory approach to learning often provides both skills improvement and compensation for weaknesses.

Assistive Technologies

Reading

Optical Character Recognition (OCR) Systems/Speech Synthesis Systems. These "reading" machines take printed text and read it aloud to the user. It is possible to scan printed material (such as a page of a book, lecture notes, or a test) into the computer. The material is then read back to the user with the speech synthesis/screen reading system. This type of technology is

> Would it be helpful if you could hear what this says as you read it? OCR may be for you.

especially useful for students who have little comprehension when reading, but who have strong comprehension when listening. Some of these systems highlight the words as they are spoken, allowing the reader to follow along.

Pen-sized scanners are also available. The user scans this portable device along a line of typed text and it can "read" a word or an entire section aloud.

Screen reading software. Special Web browsers also provide speech synthesizers that read text out loud.

Tape recorders. Basic tape recorders and variable speech control (VSC) playback varieties can be useful for both remediation and compensation. Students can strengthen reading skills by following along a printed page as the recorder plays a taped version of the text. The machine can be adjusted to play the material at a slow rate (without voice distortion) to improve comprehension.

Books on tape. Recordings for the Blind and Dyslexic (RFB&D) and the National Library Service for the Blind and Physically Handicapped (NLS) provide taped textbooks or recreational reading materials. Recorded materials as well as variable-speed tape players can be borrowed from these groups. Again, the borrowed materials can be used alone or the user can follow along in a printed text. RFB&D also provides e-text (books on a computer disc) that can be loaded into a computer with a voice synthesizer and then read to the user.

Listening and Note Taking

Tape recorders. Students who have trouble processing speech can use variable-speed players and variable-speed control players to record lectures and then listen to them at a reduced speed. For those who have problems with note taking but do not have difficulty with speech processing, the tape can be played back at a higher speed to provide a quick review of notes. Some students use the taped lectures to reinforce the information recorded with written notes.

Books on tape. Listening skills can be enhanced and improved when students listen to taped materials as they read along.

Laptop computers, small word processors, and electronic notebooks. Both laptop computers and small word processors can be used to take notes. The laptop can also store the materials. Small word processors can be plugged into personal computers to transfer the material to store or to print.

FM amplification devices. Personal FM listening devices enhance a student's ability to listen and focus. The speaker wears a small transmitter and the student wears a receiver. These systems allow the speaker's voice to be played directly into the listener's ears.

> FM amplification devices are not just for hearing impaired students. I have ADD and I use one. I have trouble concentrating and my teacher likes to move around the room. Wherever the teacher goes, his voice stays with me.
>
> —**Northern Essex Community College student**

Computer-aided real-time translation (CART). This device is used in group situations. A CART reporter types into a machine that is connected to a computer. The text is then displayed on a computer monitor or other display device for the student to read. This provides the student with the opportunity to read the information as it is presented.

Pressure-sensitive paper. A designated note taker takes notes on a carbonless paper. An easy-tear-off copy of the notes is then given to the student with note-taking problems.

Writing

Word processors/spell checkers. No technical advance has made such a difference for those with writing difficulties as the word processor. This liberating device allows students to write without worry about errors. Spell checkers and grammar checkers provide assistance and the reorganization of information can be accomplished with a few clicks. A variety of spell checker options is available. Some highlight spelling mistakes as the user types, others correct selected words automatically, and some allow for checking after the document is completed.

In addition to word processing programs available on personal computers, portable word processors are also available. They are less expensive than laptop computers and provide word processing programs that may include spell checking and printing options.

Organization software for writing (brainstorming/outlining). Many of today's word processing programs include organizational software that allows students to pour information from their heads onto the page without worrying about organization. The software can provide an outline to help reorganize the material once it is put onto the page. Some programs automatically create Roman numerals for heading, and letters and numbers for subheadings.

Some programs provide diagrams to help with organization. This type of information mapping or webbing can help the student organize information as he or she brainstorms ideas. Once complete, the graphic organizer can automatically convert the information into a traditional outline form.

Many word processing programs provide templates or samples of forms, applications, letters, and similar formats that can help with the organizational component of writing.

Word prediction software. Software programs can also reduce the time necessary by predicting the word the user is typing and completing it. After the user types a few letters, the program predicts what the word might be and provides a list of options. The writer can then point and click on the appropriate word. Words can be added to the software database, and in some cases, abbreviations for frequently used words can also be added. Since the software can reduce the number of keystrokes necessary to complete a document, it can be a real timesaver. It provides correct spelling, and since the writer must identify the correct word, he or she gets a visual reminder of the correct spelling. It can also help provide a prompt for a student who might be stuck for a word.

> Are your verbal skills strong?
>
> Do you get your message across best when you speak rather than write?
>
> A speech recognition program may help you improve your writing.

Speech recognition. Students with strong verbal skills but poor writing skills may benefit from speech recognition programs. The writer uses a microphone and dictates what he or she would like to write as the program converts the spoken word into text. If the selected text is incorrect, it will provide a list of similar sounding words as alternatives. Some programs require a pause between words, others respond at a normal conversational pace. Most allow for both keyboard or voice-activated editing. The programs learn the phonetic characteristics of the user's voice and improve with use.

Speech synthesis—text to speech. In just the opposite of the speech recognition program, speech synthesis allows users to hear what they are writing. As the writer types the information, the voice synthesizer reads the information. The programs can highlight and read as the user types, or the material can be read back in sections or after the document is complete.

Tape recorders. Some students don't need speech recognition software, but can benefit from dictating their ideas into a tape recorder and then playing them back as they type the information into the word processor. For them, their verbal skills can help them get their ideas out and the recorder can hold the ideas for them until they can put them on paper.

Math

Calculators. A variety of calculators can help student with weaknesses in math. Traditional calculators can help with basic mathematical functions. Some calculators now come with special features that provide both visual and audio displays and some respond to spoken input. For some, large screen displays or large buttons on the keypad can also help. Most computers come with an onscreen calculator and some have speech components as well.

Checkbook programs. In the basic survival/life skills category, there are many software programs available to help with balancing checkbooks.

Software. Unfortunately, much of the mathematics software available is intended to teach or reinforce basic skills and is intended for a younger market.

Organizing/Time Management

Data managers/day planners/organizers. Many people use data organizers to help them keep track of their plans and activities. For those with learning disabilities, these devices are a solid tool. Data managers can be installed in personal computers and are available as portable devices. Some are even voice activated. They can store messages, reminders, schedules, and so on. They come with calendars, address books, and phone directories. Some also have clocks and alarms. Some include dictionaries and/or spell checkers.

Free-form databases. Individualized database systems can be used with personal computers to store notes and reminders. This type of software can store and retrieve notes of any length. The user can call up information by typing a "keyword" if the user can remember only part of the information. It is also possible to browse through notes in the database.

Watches. New, specialized watches not only keep track of time but can be programmed to sound a reminder alarm or vibration many times during the day. They can be used in a variety of ways. They may be used to remind students to get back on task. They can be used to remind students to get ready for an appointment. They can be preset for the amount of time to be devoted to work or to a section of a test. The options for use are as individual as the wearer.

Social skills. Nothing improves social skills like practice, practice, and practice. There are not many software or CD-ROM programs available to help young adults with social skills, but there are some. Some provide role-playing opportunities in real-life situations and can help with decision-making skills. Others are job related and can help users learn to take messages, request information, make introductions, ask for help, accept criticism, apologize, or prioritize parts of a job. A Web search with the key words "social skills software" can help you find specific software programs.

Resources

To comply with federal regulations, states have set up assistive technology projects. Some offer guidance, some offer equipment on loan, some offer evaluations and training, and some offer demonstration centers. To find out what is available in your state, call your state department of education, or follow the links on the Tech Act Projects List on the ABLEDATA Web site listed below.

National Institute on Disability and Rehabilitation Research
http://www.abledata.com/Site_2/state_technology_assistance_proj.htm

Alliance for Technology Access (ATA)
http://www.ataccess.org

Computer and Web Resources for People with Disabilities. 3rd ed.
Alameda, Calif.: Hunter House, 2000.

Georgia's Technology Assistance Information Page, Learning
Disabilities and Assistive Technologies
http://www.gatfl.org/ldguide/terms.htm
Incorporates an assistive technology evaluation and information
on specific difficulties (i.e., reading, writing, memory organization,
and math).

LDOnline
Tech Guide
http://www.ldonline.org/ld_indepth/technology/techguide.html

The Learning Disabilities Association
Educational Technology & Learning Disabilities
http://www.ldanatl.org/
(800) 300-6710

Recording for the Blind and Dyslexic (RFB&D)
http://www.rfbd.org/
(800) 221-4792 (for individual memberships)
Schools usually have memberships and can order materials for you.

National Library Services for the Blind and Physically Handicapped
http://lcweb.loc.gov/nls/nls.html
(800) 424-8567

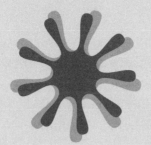

Glossary

accommodations: techniques, materials, and/or equipment that provide slight differences in the way information is presented, making it easier for students with learning disabilities to learn

ACT: a national college admissions exam that consists of tests in English, reading, mathematics, and scientific reasoning

age-equivalent: the average score that a child in a particular age would get on a test

agraphia: a term used to describe student with deficits in written language

amphetamines: a medication that can decrease impulsivity and hyperactivity and improve attention (e.g., Dexedrine, Dextrostat, or Adderall)

Asperger's syndrome: a developmental disorder that affects a person's ability to understand and socially interact with other people. A form of high-functioning autism.

assessment: a test used to determine the need for special education services

assistive technology: any piece of equipment that allows learning disabled students to increase, maintain, or improve their functional capabilities while doing school or work tasks

attention deficit hyperactivity disorder (ADHD): a neurobiological disorder that includes a combination of inattentive, hyperactive, and impulsive behaviors that are developmentally inappropriate and severe enough to impair function at home and school

attention span: the amount of time you can stay with a certain task without being distracted

auditory ability: the ability to distinguish sounds and to understand the symbols associated with those sounds

auditory processing: being able to understand and integrate spoken information, words, or sounds

autism: a syndrome that is characterized by impaired social interaction, problems with verbal and nonverbal communication and imagination, unusual or severely limited activities and interests, and the inability to understand another person's perspective

automaticity: the ability to recall and use information quickly

axon: the part of the neuron that carries outgoing signals away from the cell body

basal ganglion: the processing center of the brain, located deep inside the cerebrum, important for controlling movement

brain injured: damage to brain tissue. The term was often misused in the '30s and '40s to describe children with learning problems.

brain stem: the part of the brain that connects the cerebrum to the spinal cord and controls functions necessary for survival, such as breathing, heart rate, blood pressure, and digestion

cerebellum: located at the base of the back of the brain, this section controls balance, coordination, and movement

cerebrum: the part of the brain that is made up of the frontal lobe, the parietal lobe, the temporal lobe, and the occipital lobe. It plays a role in hearing, vision, the perception of touch (pressure, temperature, and pain), reasoning, planning, parts of speech, movement, emotions, and problem solving. It is divided into halves or cerebral hemispheres.

chronological age: your actual age in years

chunking: breaking down information into small and meaningful parts in order to make sense of it

cognitive abilities: your ability to learn, which is related to intelligence

compensation: using a strong ability to cover for a weak one

corpus callosum: a thick band of fibers that connects right and left brain hemispheres to allow for communication between the two sides

Dalcroze training: a form of music education developed by Emile Jacques-Dalcroze that is based on movement in response to music. It is sometimes called eurythmics.

deficit: an area of difficulty that interferes with your learning

dendrite: the part of the neuron that detects signals from another cell

discrepancy: a significant difference between two areas of functioning

distractibility: the inability to attend to a task at hand

dopamine: a brain chemical that is transferred from one cell to another through neural networks in the brain and that has been associated with movement, thought, motivation, and pleasure

dyscalculia: a mathematical learning disability in which a person with normal or above-average intelligence has unusual difficulty solving arithmetic problems and grasping math concepts

dysgraphia: difficulty with handwriting when a student has no physical impairments, and his or her writing ability falls substantially below expectations, despite average to above-average intelligence

dyslexia: a disorder manifested by difficulty in learning to read despite conventional instruction, adequate intelligence, and sociocultural opportunity. It may affect listening, speaking, reading, writing, and spelling.

dyslexia dysgraphia: a learning disability characterized by illegible writing and poor oral spelling

episodic memory: recall based on past events, often enhanced by sensory input such as sights, sounds, and smells

executive functions: the brain functions that allow planning, organization, and the development of strategies for problem solving

expressive language: the ability to communicate with others through speaking, writing, or gestures

free and appropriate education: the federal designation that provides opportunities for learning disabled children to receive the services they need in the regular classroom, sometimes with additional support outside the classroom

frontal lobe: the region of brain that determines your personality and emotions. It is important for reasoning, judgment, organization, impulses, emotions, problem solving, sexual behavior, language, and movement

functional Magnetic Resonance Imaging (fMRI): a brain imaging technique that records changes in the natural magnetic properties of blood cells that carry oxygen

graphic organizers: a linear or pictorial template for organizing written information

gray matter: a mass of neurons

heredity: the genetic transmission of qualities that are passed on from parents to children

hyperactivity: excessive and almost constant movement that can interfere with your ability to learn new information and with social interactions

impulsivity: the tendency to act or speak quickly without thinking about the consequences

individualized education plan (IEP): the document that the special education team develops, listing areas of strength, areas of weakness, and the types of help a student will need to succeed in school

internalized speech: talking to ourselves silently, in our minds

kinesthetic: the sense of touch that is used to help you learn

learning disabilities: a term used to describe any number of problems that make it difficult to learn

least restrictive environment: an educational setting where students who need special education services are, to the greatest extent possible, educated with students who do not need special education services

left hemisphere of the brain: the side of the brain that usually controls the right side of the body, language, mathematics, abstraction, and reasoning and cognitive functions

limbic system: areas of the brain that interact with other parts of the brain to form memories and emotional responses. It also is involved with other sensory parts of the brain.

long-term memory: information that is stored in your brain that can be retrieved and used at a later time

mainstreaming: including students who need special education services in regular education classes

minimal brain dysfunction syndrome: term used in the past to refer to children with learning problems

modality: the sense you use to take in information and learn, that is, either through visual, auditory, or kinesthetic (sight, sound, or touch)

motor dysgraphia: a type of dysgraphia characterized by illegible writing and sometimes difficulty with drawing

motor memory: what you remember by doing; recall based on hands-on activities

motor planning: sequencing and organizing movements to perform an activity

multisensory: using more than one sense, or modality, to get information

neurons: nerve cells, dendrites, and axons that allow the parts of the brain to communicate with each other

neurotransmitters: chemicals that transmit impulses between neurons

nonverbal learning disability (NLD): a right-hemisphere brain syndrome characterized by deficits in nonverbal reasoning

objectives: the individual steps that make up the annual goals of your IEP

occipital lobe: the part of the brain where vision is processed

optical character recognition (OCR) system: a system that can scan and convert written text into computer documents and that can be read by a speech synthesis system

parietal lobe: the part of the brain between the frontal and occipital lobes that controls how we understand and process information about the environment and helps us understand what we see and feel

percentiles: a score that indicates the rank of a score as compared to others of the same age or grade

perceptually handicapped: term used in the '50s and '60s to refer to children with learning problems

phonemes: separate sounds or segments of speech

phonemic awareness: the ability to break words down into their separate sounds or segments of speech, called phonemes

phonics: a method of teaching reading by teaching the individual sounds that are represented by letters and words

positron emission tomography (PET): a brain scan that records brain activities using radioactively enhanced chemicals that are injected into the blood stream

prefrontal cortex: the front part of the frontal lobe where the higher cognitive functions are located and where executive decisions are made

premotor and motor areas: the part of the frontal lobe that controls and produces movement

primary sensory cortex: the part of the parietal lobe that controls sensation (touch, pressure)

procedural memory: what you remember by doing; motor memory, developed by hands-on activities

psychological tests: evaluations done by a psychologist that look at your cognitive ability, how you learn, and at any emotional issues you might have

rapid naming: the ability to quickly access and retrieve verbal labels for visual information

reasonable accommodations: educational changes and strategies designed to help students with learning disabilities

recognition memory: information that is remembered with the help of clues or hints

reconstitution: the ability to break down things that we have learned in the past and then reorder them in a way that helps us create new ideas

reflexive memory: an automatic reaction that you use when you are recalling information you know really well

resource room: a place outside the regular classroom where you can receive specific special education services

right hemisphere of the brain: the side of the brain that controls the left side of the body and is in charge of nonverbal processes, such as attention, pattern recognition, line orientation, and the detection of complex sounds

Ritalin: the trade name for one of the stimulant drugs used to treat ADHD

SAT: Scholastic Aptitude Tests: tests that provide colleges with information about the likelihood of college success

self-monitoring: the ability to notice mistakes and correct them without outside help

self-regulation: the ability to control emotions

semantic memory: memory based on words: names, facts, figures, and so on

sensory integration: a neurobiological process allowing the organization and understanding of information gathered through touch (pressure, temperature, pain), movement, and body awareness

short-term memory: the information that is held from one to two seconds while the brain decides whether to keep it, store it, or discard it

single photon emission computed tomography (SPECT): a brain scan that uses radioactive tracers and a scanner to record the brain activity. Computers process the information and create images showing details of brain function.

spatial dysgraphia: problems understanding space that contribute to illegible writing and problems with drawing

spatial organization: the ability to understand and relate to the surrounding space

special education: specifically designed instruction intended to meet the individual needs of students with special needs

stimulant medication: a medication that can decrease impulsivity and hyperactivity and improve attention (e.g., methylphenidate [Ritalin])

synapse: the place of contact between the axon of one cell and a dendrite of another

synaptic gap: the space between neurons, which is a distance much smaller than a thousandth of a millimeter

syntax: the order for words in a sentence

temporal lobe: the region on each cerebral hemisphere that controls hearing and the ability to recognize words and is involved with short- and long-term memory

transition period: the passage from high school to life after high school, or the time you spend preparing for what you will do after high school graduation

transitional plan: focuses on post–high school goals and the skills and programs needed to meet goals; sometimes called transitional IEP (TIEP) or individualized transition plan (ITP)

visual processing: how we understand how objects relate to each other in space

visual-spatial problems: difficulty recognizing your own body's position in space

white matter: the pathways that connect different parts of the brain

word blindness: a term once used to describe those who had difficulty learning to read

working memory: the thoughts and information we can hold onto temporarily while problems are solved

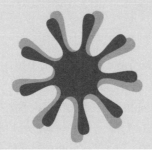

Sources

Chapter 1—Learning Disabilities: An Overview

"General Information Packet on Learning Disabilities." *National Center for Learning Disabilities* <http://www.ncld.org/brochures/geninfo.html> [accessed 27 March 2000].

Hallahan, Daniel P., and James M. Kauffman. *Exceptional Children: Introduction to Special Education.* Boston: Allyn and Bacon, 1991.

Koch, John. "The Interview by John Koch: Jonathan Mooney." *The Boston Globe Magazine* (26 November 2000).

"Learning Disabilities." *National Institute of Mental Health* <http://www.nimn.nih.gov/publicat/learndis.htm> [accessed19 October 2000].

Lerner, Janet W. *Children with Learning Disabilities.* New York: Houghton Mifflin, 1971.

Mooney, Jonathan. *Learning Outside the Lines: Two Ivy League Students with Learning Disabilities and ADHD Give You the Tools for Academic Success and Educational Revolution.* New York: Simon & Schuster, 2000.

National Center for Learning Disabilities. <http://www.ncld.org/index.html> [accessed 2 May 2001].

Newman, Renee M. "Dyslexia: Technology for Compliance with Federal Special Ed Laws." *Dyscalculia.org* <http://www.dyscalculia.org/edu504.html, 1998> [accessed 16 April 2001].

Opp, G. "Historical Roots of the Field of Learning Disabilities: Some Nineteenth-Century German Contributions." *Journal of Learning Disabilities* (January 1994).

Zametkin, Alan J. "Hyperactivity." *Hyperactivity* (1995).

Chapter 2—Your Brain

Amen, Daniel G., M.D. *Images into the Mind: A Radical New Look at Understanding and Changing Behavior.* Fairfield, Calif.: Mindworks Press, 1995.

Barkley, Russell A. "Attention Deficit Hyperactivity Disorder." *Scientific American* (September 1998).

Begley, Sharon. "Getting Inside a Teen Brain." *Newsweek* (28 February 2000).

———. "A World of Their Own." *Newsweek* (8 May 2000).

"Brain Salad." *NLD on the Web* <http://www.nldontheweb.org/brain_salad.htm>. (accessed 29 January 2001)

"Brain Scan May Help Diagnose ADHD." *MSNBC* <http://www.msnbc.com/news/347444.asp> 16 December 1999 [accessed 9 November 2000].

"Dysfunctional Network in Brain's Left Hemisphere Linked to Dyslexia." *National Institute of Mental Health* <http://www.nimh.nih.gov/events/prleftdy.htm> 20 July 1998 [accessed 10 October 2000].

"Examining the Emergence of Brain Development Research." *Childhood Education* (fall 1999).

"fMRI Reveals Dynamics of Working Memory." *National Institute of Mental Health* <http://www.nimh.nih.gov/events/prfmri1.cfm> 9 September 1999 [accessed 17 July 2000].

Guyer, Ruth Levy. "fMRI: Pictures of the Brain in Action." *Research in the News, National Institutes of Health* <http://science-education.nih.gov/snapshots.nsf/story?openform&rtn~ SB_Dyslexia_fMRI> 26 October 1998 [accessed 8 January 2001].

Levine, Mel. *All Kinds of Minds.* Cambridge, Mass.: Educators Publishers, 1993.

Mathias, Robert. "The Basics of Brain Imagine." *NIDA Notes* 11, no. 5. <http://www.nida.nih.gov/NIDA_Notes/NNVol11N5/Basics.html> November/December 1996 [accessed 8 January 2001].

"Memory and Recall." *Math Matters* <www.mathmatters.net/memory.html> June 1998 [accessed 5 December 2000].

"Our Perspective: A Neurodevelopmental View." *All Kinds of Minds* <www.allkindsofminds.org/perspective/neuroView.htm> 2000 [accessed 11 October 2000].

Ratey, John. *A User's Guide to the Brain.* New York: Pantheon, 2001.

Seltz, Johanna. "Teen Brains Are Different." *The Boston Sunday Globe* (28 May 2000).

Shaywitz, Sally E., Bennett A. Shaywitz, et al. "Functional Disruption in the Organization of the Brain for Reading in Dyslexia." Proceedings of the National Academy of Science, March 1998.

"Subtle Brain Circuit Abnormalities Confirmed in ADHD." *National Institute of Mental Health* <www.nimh.nih.gov/events/pradhd.htm> 16 July 1996 [accessed 17 July 2000].

Swanson, James, and F. Xavier Castellanos, M.D. "Biological Bases of Attention Deficit Hyperactivity Disorder: Neuroanatomy, Genetics, and Pathophysiology." <http://add.about.com/health/add/library/weekly/aa1119c.htm> [accessed November 2000].

"Teenage Brain: A Work in Progress." *National Institute of Mental Health* <http://www.nimh.nih.gov/publicat/teenbrain.cfm> January 2001 [accessed 2 May 2001].

Young, Maxine. "Working Memory, Language, and Reading." *The Brain Connection, Scientific Learning* <http://www.brainconnection.com/topics/?main=fa/memory-language3> May 2000 [accessed 2 May 2001].

Chapter 3—Attention Deficit Hyperactivity Disorder

"Attention Deficit Hyperactivity Disorder (ADHD)—Questions and Answers." *National Institute of Mental Health* <http://www.nimn.nih.gov/publicat/adhdqa.cfm> April 2000 [accessed 30 October 2000].

Barkley, Russell A. "*ADHD and the Nature of Self-Control.*" New York: Guilford Press, 1997.

———. "Attention-Deficit/Hyperactivity Disorder, Self-regulation, and Time: Toward a More Comprehensive Theory." *Journal of Developmental and Behavioral Pediatrics* (August 1997).

———. "Behavioral Inhibition, Sustained Attention, and Executive Functions: Constructing a Unifying Theory of ADHD." *Psychological Bulletin* (January 1997).

———. "Attention Deficit Hyperactivity Disorder." *Scientific American* (September 1998).

———. "Genetics of Childhood Disorders: XVII. ADHD, Part 1: The Executive Functions and ADHD." *Journal of American Academy of Child and Adolescent Psychiatry* (August 2000).

Barkley, R., K. Murphy, and D. Kwasnik. "Vehicle Driving Competencies and Risks in Teens and Young Adults with Attention Deficit Hyperactivity Disorder. *Pediatrics* 98 (December 1996).

Beckley, Dawn. "Gifted and Learning Disabled: Twice Exceptional Students." *National Research Center on the Gifted and Talented* <http://www.sp.ucon.edu/~nrcgt/news/spring98/sprng984.html> 1998 winter newsletter [accessed 2 November 2000].

Brody, Linda E., and Carol J. Mills. "Gifted Children with Learning Disabilities: A Review of the Issues." *Journal of Learning Disabilities* (May/June 1997).

Cramond, Bonnie. "The Coincidence of Attention Deficit Hyperactivity Disorder." *National Resource Center for the Gifted and Talented* <http://borntoexplore.org/adhd.htm> 1995 [accessed 17 November 2000].

Crist, James. J. "ADHD: A Teenager's Guide." *National Attention Deficit Disorder Association (ADDA)* <http://www.add.org/content/teens/tguide/htm> [accessed 30 October 2000].

"Diagnosis and Treatment of Attention Deficit Hyperactivity Disorder." National Institute of Health Consensus Development Conference Statement <http://odp.od.nih.gov/consensus/> 16–18 November 1998 [accessed 30 March 1999].

Grafman, Jordan, and Irene Litvan. "Importance of Deficits in Executive Functions." *The Lancet* (London, 4 December 1999).

Finn, Jon. "Jamming with ADD: For guitarists, Is Attention Deficit Disorder a Boon or a Burden." *Attention Deficit Disorder with Bob Seay* <http://www.add.about.com/health/add/library/weekly/aa110498.htm> [accessed 6 November 2000].

Gantos, Jack. *Joey Pigza Swallowed the Key.* New York: Farrar, Straus, & Giroux, 1998.

Garfinkel, Perry. "Making a Plus from the Deficit in A.D.D." *The New York Times* (31 October 2000).

Grafman, J., and Irene Litvan. "Importance of Deficits in Executive Functions." *The Lancet* (4 December 1999).

Hartmann, Thom. *ADD Success Stories: A Guide to Fulfillment for Families with Attention Deficit Disorder*. Grass Valley, Calif.: Underwood Books, 1995.

Ramundo, Kelly, Kate Ramundo, and Peggy Ramundo Kelly. *The ADDed Dimension: Celebrating the Opportunities, Rewards and Challenges of the ADD Experience*. New York: Fireside, 1997.

Seay, Bob. "The ADDed Brain: A Biological Marker for ADHD." <http://add.about.com/health/add/library/weekly/blad-dmri.htm> 23 November 1998 [accessed 6 November 2000].

Skoff, Barry. "The Role of Executive Functions in ADHD and Learning Disabilities." *LDAM Gazette*, The Journal of Learning Disabilities Association of Massachusetts (April 2000).

Swanson, James, and F. Xavier Castellanos, M.D. "Biological Bases of Attention Deficit Hyperactivity Disorder: Neuroanatomy, Genetics, and Pathophysiology." <http://add.about.com/health/add/library/weekly/aa1119c.htm> [accessed 6 November 2000].

Swanson, J. M., et al. "Attention-Deficit Hyperactivity Disorder and Hyperkinetic Disorder." *The Lancet* (7 February 1998).

Talan, Jamie. "Biology of Behavior: The Possible Link between Genes, Attention Deficit." *Newsday* (22 December 1998).

Weirs, Reinout, W. W. Boudewijn Gunning, and Joseph A. Sergeant. "Is a Mild Deficit in Executive Functions in Boys Related to Childhood ADHD or to Parental Multigenerational Alcoholism?" *Journal of Abnormal Child Psychology* (December 1998).

Chapter 4—Dyscalculia

Cheakalos, Christina, et al. "Heavy Mettle: They May Have Trouble Reading and Spelling, but Those with the Grit to Overcome Learning Disabilities Like Dyslexia Emerge Fortified for Life." *People Weekly* (30 October 2000).

Geary, David C. "Mathematical Disorders: An Overview for Educators." *Perspectives*, The International Dyslexia Association (summer 2000).

———. "Mathematical Disabilities: What We Know and Don't Know." *LDOnline* <www.ldonline.com/ld_indepth/math_skills/geary_math_dis.html> [accessed 9 January 01].

Hughes, Slema, and Rosemarie Kolstad. "Dyscalculia and Mathematics Achievement." *Journal of Instructional Psychology* (March 1994).

Jones, Eric E., Rich Wilson, and Shalina Bhojwani. "Mathematics Instruction for Secondary Students with Learning Disabilities." *Journal of Learning Disabilities* (March/April 1997).

Miller, Susan Peterson, and Cecil D. Mercer. "Educational Aspects of Mathematics Disabilities." *Journal of Learning Disabilities* (January/February 1997).

Shalev, R. S., O. Manor, J. Auerbach, and V. Tsur-Gross. "Persistence of Developmental Dyscalculia: What Counts?" *Journal of Pediatrics* (September 1998).

Shalev, Ruth S. "Developmental Dyscalculia Is a Familial Learning Disability." *Journal of Learning Disabilities* (January/February 2001).

Chapter 5—Dysgraphia

abcNEWS.com. On-line interview with Dr. Fred Epstein. <http://more.abcnews.go.com/sections/nightline/nightline/n1010104_epstein_mailform.html> [accessed 10 January 2001].

Avi. "Questions and Answers about Avi." *Avi's Homepage* <http://www.avi-writer.com> [accessed 3 March 2001].

Beringer, Virginia. "The Write Stuff for Preventing and Treating Disabilities." *Perspectives*, International Dyslexia Association (spring 1999).

Chadbourne, Robert D. "Road to Rhodes Had a Rocky Beginning." *The Washington Post* (29 March 2000).

"Connecting with Patients: A Q&A with Dr. Fred Epstein." <http://www.abcNEWS.com> (7 June 2001) [accessed 10 January 2001].

"Dysgraphia, Just the Facts . . . Fact Sheet #982." Baltimore, Md.: International Dyslexia Association (January 2000).

Polacco, Patricia. "A Chance to Soar." *Instuctor* (January 2001).

"Scholastic's Authors On-Line Interviews." *Scholastic's Tab Teen Book Club* <http://teacher.scholastic.com/authorsandbooks/authors/avi/interview.htm> [accessed 3 March 2001].

Chapter 6—Dyslexia

"ABCs of Dyslexia." *The International Dyslexia Association* <http://www.interdys.org/abcsofdyslexia/page4.asp> [accessed 4 January 2001].

"Atypical Brain Activity Detected in People with Dyslexia." *National Institute of Mental Health* <http://www.nimh.nih.gov/events/prdyslex.htm> [accessed 9 November 2000].

Bower, Bruce. "Moving Clues to Dyslexia." *Science News* (12 September 1998).

"Brain Research and Reading." *SchwabLearning.org* <http://64.152.66.161/Articles.asp?r=35> [accessed 6 January 2001].

Brinckerhoff, Loring "Tuning In to Taped Textbooks before College." <http://www.ldreport.com/sample_articles.htm> [accessed 5 March 2001].

Cannell, Stephen. "A Writing Fool." *Newsweek* (22 November 1999).

Davis, Ronald D. *The Gift of Dyslexia*. New York: Berkley, 1997.

Dunham, Will. "Study Establishes Dyslexia's Neurological Basis." *Science News* (15 March 2001).

"Dyslexia." *National Institute of Child Health and Human Development* (NICHD), 1995.

"Dyslexia." *National Institutes of Health,* 1995.

"Dyslexia Gene." *Lancet* (11 September 1999).

"Dyslexia the Gift." *Davis Dyslexia Association International* <http://www.dyslexia.com/> [accessed 4 May 2001].

"Educational Services Committee, Fact Sheet: Dyslexia." *Learning Disabilities Association* <http://www.ldanatl.org/factsheets/Dyslexia.shtml> May 1996 [accessed 5 January 2001].

"The Feeling Box Session, 1998 Teen Conference." *LDOnline* <http://www.ldteens.org/FeelingBox.html> [accessed 9 January 2001].

Frost, Julie A., and Michael J. Emery. "Academic Interventions for Children with Dyslexia Who Have Phonological Core Deficits." The Eric Clearinghouse on Disabilities and Gifted Education, ERIC Digest #E539 (August 1995).

"General Information about Dyslexia." *LDOnline* <http://ldonline.org/ld_indepth/reading/reading-4.html> [accessed 4 January 2001].

Kantrowitz, Barbara, Anne Underwood, and Pat Wingert. "Dyslexia and the New Science of Reading." *Newsweek* (22 November 1999).

Levine, Mel. *Educational Care: A System for Understanding and Helping Children with Learning Problems at Home and in School.* Cambridge, Mass.: Educators Publishing Service, 1997.

Mooney, Jonathan, and David Cole. *Learning Outside the Lines: Two Ivy League Students with Learning Disabilities and ADHD Give You the Tools for Academic Success and Educational Revolution.* New York: Fireside, 2000.

Mulligan, Kelly. "Brokovich Emphasizes Concern for Others." *The Digital Collegean* (13 September 2000, Penn State's Distinguished Speaker Series).

"NICHD-Funded Researchers Map Physical Basis of Dyslexia." *National Institute of Child Health and Human Development* <http://156.40.88.3/new/releases/dyslexianews.htm> March 1998 [accessed 5 January 2001].

Shapiro, Joan, and Rebecca Rich. *Facing Learning Disabilities in the Adult Years: Understanding Dyslexia, ADHD, Assessment, Intervention, and Research.* New York: Oxford University Press, 1999.

Shaywitz, Sally E., Bennett A. Shaywitz, et al. "Functional Disruption in the Organization of the Brain for Reading in Dyslexia." Proceedings of the National Academy of Science, March 1998.

Underwood, Anne. "New Clues to the Puzzle of Dyslexia." *Newsweek* (7 June 1999).

Young, Maxine L. "Working Memory, Language and Reading." *Scientific Learning Corporation* <http://www.brainconnection.com/topics/ ?main=fa/memory-language3> [accessed 3 May 2001].

Wolfe, Maryanne, and Patricia G. Bowers. "Naming-Speed Processes and Developmental Reading Disabilities: An Introduction to the Special Issue on the Double-Deficit Hypothesis." *Journal of Learning Disabilities* (July/August 2000).

Chapter 7—Foreign Languages

Barr, Vickie. "Foreign Language Requirements and Students with Learning Disabilities." Washington, D.C., ERIC Clearinghouse on Languages and Linguistics, reprinted with changes from an article that appeared in the September-October 1992 issue of *Information for Heath.* Washington, D.C., Heath Resource Center <http://ericae.net/edo/ED355834.htm> [accessed 22 February 2001].

Ganschow, Leonore, and Richard Sparks. "Foreign Language Learning Difficulties: An Historical Perspective." *Journal of Learning Disabilities* (May/June 1998).

Marcos, Kathleen M. "Second Language Learning: Everyone Can Benefit." *The Eric Review* <http://www.accesseric.org/resources/ ericreview/vol6no1/langlern.html> [accessed 16 March 2001].

Moore, Francis X. "Section 504 of the Americans for Disabilities Act: Accommodating the Learning Disabled Student in the Foreign Language Curriculum." *ADFL Bulletin* (winter 1995).

Schwarz, Robin L. "Learning Disabilities and Foreign Language Learning: A Painful Collision." *LDOnline* <http://www.ldonline.org/ld_indepth/foreign_language_lang/painful_collision.html> October 1997 [accessed 3 September 2001].

Scott, Sally S., and Elaine Manglitz. "Foreign Language Learning and Learning Disabilities: Making the College Transition." *Their World*. New York: National Center for Learning Disabilities, 2000.

Chapter 8—Nonverbal Learning Disability

Dimitrovsky, Lilly, Hedva Spector, Rachel Levy-Shiff, and Eli Vakil. "Interpretation of Facial Expressions of Affect in Children with Learning Disabilities with Verbal or Nonverbal Deficits." *Journal of Learning Disabilities* (May/June 1998).

Foss, Jean. "Nonverbal Learning Disabilities and Remedial Interventions." *Annals of Dyslexia* 41 (The Orton Dyslexia Society, 1991).

Frankenberger, Caryl. "Non-Verbal Learning Disabilities: An Emerging Profile." *NLDline* <http://www.nldline.com/frannkenb.htm> [accessed 22 November 2000].

Fudge, Emily S. "What Is Nonverbal Learning Disorder Syndrome?" *Asperger Syndrome Coalition of the United States* <http://www.asperger.org/articles/nld003.asp> [accessed 22 November 2000].

Green, Deborah. *Growing Up with NLD*. Albuquerque, N.M.: Silicon Heights Computers, 2000.

Harnadek, Michael, and Byron P. Rourke. "Principal Identifying Features of the Syndrome of Nonverbal Learning Disabilities in Children." *Journal of Learning Disabilities* (March 1994).

Levine, Mel. *Educational Care: A System for Understanding and Helping Children with Learning Problems at Home and In School*. Cambridge, Mass.: Educators Publishing Service, 1994.

Roman, Michael. "The Syndrome of Nonverbal Learning Disabilities: Clinical Description and Applied Aspects." *Current Issues in Education* (fall 1998) (reprinted with permission on *LDOnline*). <http://www.ldonline.org/ld_indepth/nonverbal/syndrome_of _nonverbal_ld.html> [accessed 7 November 2000].

Rourke, Byron P. *Nonverbal Learning Disabilities: The Syndrome and the Model*. New York: Guilford Press, 1989.

"Tera's NLD Jumpstation: A Resource on Nonverbal Learning Disabilities by an NLD Person." <http://www.geocities.com/ HotSprings/Spa/7262> [accessed 4 May 2001].

Thompson, Sue. "Nonverbal Learning Disorders." *NLDline* <www. nldline.com/nld_sue.htm>.

———. *The Source for Nonverbal Learning Disorders*. East Moline, Ill.: LinguiSystems, 1997.

Chapter 9—Your Test Report

"Psycho-Educational Evaluations." *Psychological Services, Fairleigh Dickinson University* <http://www.fdu.edu/centers/cps/ psychoedevals.html> [accessed 10 April 2001].

Chapter 10—The IEP

"Helping Students Develop Their IEPs." *National Information Center for Youth and Disabilities* (NICHCY) (December 1995).

"How to Participate Effectively in the IEP Process." *Learning Disabilities Association of America*.

Lovitt, Thomas C. "High School Students Rate Their IEPs: Low Opinions and Lack of Ownership." *Intervention in School and Clinic* (September 1994).

Peters, Mary. T. "Someone's Missing." *Preventing School Failure* (summer 1990).

"Student's Guide to the IEP." Washington, D.C.: National Information Center for Children and Youth with Disabilities (NICHCY), 1995.

Chapter 11—Transition Planning

Brinckerhoff, Loring C. "Making the Transition to Higher Education." *Journal of Learning Disabilities* (March 1996).

Clark, Gary. "Transitional Planning Assessment for Secondary-Level Students." *Journal of Learning Disabilities* (January 1996).

DeFur, Sharon H. "Transition Planning: A Team Effort." *NICHY Transition Summary.* Washington, D.C.: NICHY, 1999.

Levinson, Edward, and Denise Ohler. "Transition from High School to College for Students with Learning Disabilities." *High School Journal* (October/November 1998).

"National Joint Committee on Learning Disabilities, Secondary to Post Secondary Education Transition Planning for Students with Learning Disabilities." *LDOnline* <http://www.ldonline.org/njcld/secondary.html> January 1994 [accessed 18 July 2000].

Seay, Bob. "The Transitional IEP." *About.com. Attention Deficit Disorder* <http://add/about.com> [accessed 20 July 2000].

West, Linda, et al. "Transition and Self-Advocacy" (excerpted on LDOnline, from Integrating Transition Planning into the IEP Process, 2nd ed., Council for Exceptional Children). <http://ldonline.org> 1999 [accessed 18 July 2000].

Chapter 12—The Law and Your Rights

"ADHD—New Legal Responsibilities for Schools." *LDOnline* <http://www.ldoneline.org/ld_indepth/add_adhd/ael_legal.html> [accessed 8 February 2001].

"Auxiliary Aids and Services for Postsecondary Students with Disabilities: High Education's Obligations under Section 504 and Title II of the ADA." Washington, D.C.: U.S. Department of Education, Office for Civil Rights, September 1998.

"The Civil Rights of Students with Hidden Disabilities under Section 504 of the Rehabilitation Act of 1973." *Office for Civil Rights* <http://www.ed.gov/ocr/docs/hq5269.html> [accessed 28 January2001].

"The Education of Children and Youth with Special Needs: What Do the Laws Say?" *NICHCY News Digest* 15 (October 1996).

"Faces of ADA." *U.S. Department of Justice* <http://janweb.icdi.wvu.edu/kinder/linkframe.htm> [accessed 5 May 2001].

A Guide to Disability Rights Laws. Washington, D.C.: U.S. Department of Justice, 2000.

Henderson, Kelly. "Overview of ADA, IDEA, and Section 504." *ERIC Digest E537,* Reston, Va.: ERIC Clearing House on Disabilities and Gifted Education, 1995.

"IDEA '97 General Information: An Overview of the Bill to Provide a Broad Understanding of Some of the Changes in IDEA '97." *Department of Education* <http://www.ed.gov/offices/OSERS/IDEA/overview/html> [accessed 9 December 2001].

"IDEA '97 Training Package." *NICHCY* <http://www.nichcy.org/ideatrai.htm> 8 December 2000 [accessed 12 December 2001].

"Questions and Answers about IDEA." *NICHCY News Digest* (January 2000).

Rosenfeld, James S. "Section 504 and IDEA: Basic Similarities and Differences." *LD Online* <http://www.ldonline.org/ld_indepth/legal_legislative/edlaw504.html> [accessed 8 February 2001].

"Student Placement in Elementary and Secondary Schools and Section 504 and Title II of the Americans with Disabilities Act." *U.S. Department of Education, Office of Civil Rights* <http://www.ed.gov/ocr/docs/placpub.html> August 1998 [accessed 30 January 2001].

Chapter 13—Reviewing Postsecondary Education Options

Barr, Vickie M., Rhona C. Hartman, and Stephen A. Spillane. "Getting Ready for College: Advising High School Students with Learning Disabilities." *Amercian Council on Education, HEATH Resource Center* (spring 1995).

Berg, Adriane G. "How to Assess the Best Values among Colleges." *MSN Money Central* <http://wwwmoneycontral.msn.com> [accessed 30 March 2001].

Brinckerhoff, Loring C. "Making the Transition to Higher Education: Opportunities for Student Empowerment." *Journal of Learning Disabilities* (March 1996).

"Highlights of Full-Time College Freshmen, by Type of Disability: 1998." *American Council on Education, HEATH Resource Center* (based on unpublished data from the 1998 Cooperative Institutional Research Program, UCLA 1999).

Hishinuma, Earl S., and John S. Fremstad. "ACT and SAT Modifications: A Summary." *The International Dyslexia Association* <http://www.interdys.org> [accessed 4 April 2001].

Jarrow, Jane, et al. *How to Choose a College: Guide for the Student with a Disability*. 5th ed. Washington, D.C.: American Council on Education, HEATH Resource Center, 1997.

"Policy Statement for Documentation of a Learning Disability in Adolescents and Adults." *Educational Testing Service* <http://www.ets.org/textonly/distest/ldpolicy.html> January 1998 [accessed 31 March 2001].

"Video Vignettes of Transition Aged Students." *Massachusetts Partnership for Transition, Children's Hospital, Boston* <http://www.childrenshospital.org/ici/icinet/forum> [accessed 5 May 2001].

Welbourn, Lynn. "The College Advisor: College Admission Info on the Web." *Salem Evening News*, 28 August 2000.

Chapter 14—No More Teachers, No More Books

Americorps. <http://www.americorps.org> [accessed 4 April 2001].

Center for Interim Programs. <http://www.interimprograms.com> [accessed 2 April 2001].

Lee, Linda. *Success without College.* New York: Doubleday, 2000.

Military Career Guide. <http://www.militarycareers.com> [accessed 5 May 2001].

"Occupational Outlook Handbook." *Bureau of Labor Statistics, U.S. Department of Labor* <http://stats.bls.gov/oco/ocos249.htm> [accessed 7 April 2000].

Woods, Danielle. *The Uncollege Alternative.* New York: HarperCollins, 2000.

Chapter 15—Assistive Technology

"Considering Your Child's Need for Assistive Technology." *LD Online* <http://www.ldonline.org/ld_indepth/technology/bowzer_reed.html> [accessed 31 January 2001].

Day, Sheryl L., and Barbara Edwards. "Assistive Technology for Postsecondary Students with Learning Disabilities." *Journal of Learning Disabilities* (September 1996).

"Fact Sheet: An Assistive Technology Publication of Tools for Life." *Georgia's Technology Assistance Project* <http://www.gatfl.org/ldfs/ldfactsheet.htm> [accessed 19 February 2001].

"LDA Fact Sheet: Assistive Technology for Individuals with Learning Disabilities." *Learning Disabilities Association of America* <http://www.ldanatl.org> accessed 22 February 2001].

Raskind, Marshall, and Eleanor Higgins. "Assistive Technology for Postsecondary Students with Learning Disabilities: An Overview." *LDOnline* <http://www.ldonline.org/ld_indepth/technology/raskind1.html> September 1998 (reprinted with permission on *LDOnline*) [accessed 31 January 2001].

Riviere, Adrienne. "Assistive Technology: Meeting the Needs of Adults with Learning Disabilities." National Adult Literacy and Learning Disabilities Center, *LDOnline* <http://www.ldonline.org/ld_indepth/technology/nalldc_guide.html> summer 1996 [accessed 31 January 2001].

Index

Italic numbers refer to illustrations and tables.

About the Authors

Penny Hutchins Paquette is an educational writer and former school librarian. She has wealth of experience helping teenagers people find appropriate books to help them with their concerns. This is her first book for Scarecrow's *It Happened to Me* series. Her second book in the series, *Asthma: The Ultimate Teen Guide*, will be released in 2003. In addition to writing for teenagers, she is the co-author of *Parenting a Child with a Learning Disability*, *Parenting a Child with a Behavior Problem*, and *Thinking Games to Play with Your Child*.

Cheryl Gerson Tuttle has more than thirty years of experience in the field of learning disabilities. She is a special education coordinator for the Marblehead, Massachusetts Public Schools and the co-author of four other books: *Thinking Games to Play with Your Child*, *Parenting a Child with a Learning Disability*, *Challenging Voices*, and *Parenting a Child with a Behavior Problem*.